VEGANA
ITALIANA

VEGANA ITALIANA

TRADITIONAL ITALIAN *the* PLANT-BASED WAY

TARA PUNZONE

WITH GENE STONE

RODALE

NEW YORK

Rodale Books
An imprint of Random House
A division of Penguin Random House LLC
1745 Broadway, New York, NY 10019
rodalebooks.com | randomhousebooks.com
penguinrandomhouse.com

Published in the United States by Rodale Books, an imprint of Random House, a division of Penguin Random House LLC, New York.

Rodale & Plant with colophon is a registered trademark of Penguin Random House LLC.

Family photos are from the author's collection.

Library of Congress Cataloging-in-Publication Data
Names: Punzone, Tara, author. | Stone, Gene, 1951– author.
Title: Vegana Italiana / Tara Punzone ; with Gene Stone.
Description: First edition. | New York, NY : Rodale, [2025] | Includes index.
Identifiers: LCCN 2024048886 (print) | LCCN 2024048887 (ebook) |
    ISBN 9780593736173 | ISBN 9780593736180 (ebook)
Subjects: LCSH: Vegan cooking. | Cooking, Italian.
Classification: LCC TX837 .P86 2025 (print) | LCC TX837 (ebook) |
    DDC 641.5/63620945—dc23/eng/20241205
LC record available at https://lccn.loc.gov/2024048886
LC ebook record available at https://lccn.loc.gov/2

Printed in China

9 8 7 6 5 4 3 2 1

First Edition

Editor: Katherine Leak
Art Director: Lynne Yeamans
Designer: Martha Ormiston
Managing Editor: Allison Fox
Production Editor: Cassie Gitkin
Production Manager: Jenn Backe
Photographer: Ed Anderson
Food & Prop Stylist: Valerie Aikman-Smith
Compositor: Merri Ann Morrell
Copy Editor: Martha Schwartz
Proofreaders: Regina Castillo, Marisa Crumb, Mindy Fichter,
    Russell Powers, Leda Scheintaub, Emily Zebrowski
Indexer: Gina Guilinger
Publicist: Kelly Doyle
Marketers: Danielle Kolodkin, Julia Diaz-Young

———— ◦•◦ ————

This book is dedicated to
my mother and father. My life's
purpose has always been to
make them joyful and proud.

———— ◦•◦ ————

CONTENTS

My Story **11**

The Italian Vegan Pantry **21**

Terms and Tools........................... **27**

THE BASICS

Ricotta..**32**

    Cashew Ricotta........................... **33**

    Almond Ricotta........................ **33**

Cashew Mozzarella **34**

Macadamia Parmigiano.................... **35**

Marinara Sauce **37**

Classic Pesto **38**

Pesto Calabrese........................... **39**

Pistachio Pesto............................... **41**

Roasted Pistachio Crumble................ **42**

Alfredo Sauce **44**

Gremolata **45**

Roasted Garlic **46**

Roasted Garlic Aioli........................ **48**

Cannellini Beans **49**

Pangrattato
(Italian Toasted Bread Crumbs) **51**

Chili Oil (*Olio Santo,* "Holy Oil") **52**

Grilled Ciabatta Garlic Bread............. **54**

Garlic Croutons............................. **55**

Cashew Cream.............................. **56**

Spiced Pepitas **57**

ANTIPASTI

Baked Ricotta
Served with Grilled Ciabatta **60**

Marinated Olives **62**

Olive Tapenade **63**

Castelvetrano Olive Tapenade **63**

Bruschetta **64**

Grilled Citrus Herb Tofu **67**

Gigante Beans............................... **68**

Polpettine (Meatballs)...................... **69**

Arancini...................................... **71**

Garlic Parmigiano Potato Wedges......... **75**

Crocchette di Patate **76**

Calabrian Stuffed Cherry Peppers......... **78**

Crostini...................................... **79**

   Strawberry Almond
   Ricotta Crostini **80**

   Sicilian Tuna Crostini.................... **83**

Tuna Salad................................... **84**

Stuffed Mushrooms Oreganata............ **85**

Roasted Garlic Cannellini Bean Dip **86**

INSALATA E VERDURE

Caprese **90**

Tricolore **93**

Cesare....................................... **94**

Verde **97**

Panzanella................................... **99**

Heirloom Tomato and
Watermelon Salad.......................... **100**

Broccoli Rabe............................... **102**

Sautéed Spinach............................ **103**

Sautéed Swiss Chard
with Cannellini Beans...................... **105**

Peppas **106**

Grilled Broccolini **109**

Calabrian Peppers and Potatoes.......... **110**

Candied Brussels Sprouts................. **111**

Roasted Heirloom Cauliflower............ **112**

Roasted Lemon Asparagus................ **115**

Stuffed Artichokes.......................... **116**

Roasted Winter Vegetables **120**

Grilled Summer Vegetables............... **121**

SOUPS

Pasta e Fagioli.............................. **124**

Minestrone **125**

Giambotta **126**

Escarole and Beans........................ **128**

Butternut Squash Bisque.................. **129**

Italian Wedding Soup....................... **131**

Sicilian Red Lentil Soup................... **132**

Umbrian Lentil Soup....................... **133**

Roasted Garlic Creamy
Tomato Soup **134**

PASTA

Fresh Pasta 139

Pasta Pomodoro 143

Fresh Ravioli 144

Ravioli Pomodoro 147

Fresh Gnocchi 148

Gnocchi alla Sorrentina 150

Spinach Ricotta Cannelloni 153

Lasagna Pura 155

Spaghetti Aglio, Olio e Peperoncino.... 159

Cacio e Pepe 161

Spaghetti alla Puttanesca 162

Penne all'Arrabbiata 165

Pesto Cavatelli 167

Pesto Calabrese with Bucatini 168

Fettuccine Alfredo 170

Lemon Pepper Cream Paccheri
with Spring Peas and Pistachio 173

Tagliatelle in Butternut Cream
Sauce 175

Linguine di Mare in
Garlic White Wine Sauce 177

Penne alla Vodka 181

Pasta e Ceci 183

Fusilli Primavera 184

Tagliatelle alla Bolognese 186

Baked Ziti 188

  Baked Ziti "Traditional" 189

  Baked Ziti Alfredo 190

I SECONDI

Eggplant Parmigiana 194

  Parmigiana di Melanzane 195

  Breaded Eggplant Parmigiana 196

Eggplant Parmigiana Hero 199

Meatball Parmigiana Hero 201

Grilled Tofu Panini,
aka Angelica's Panini 202

Sicilian Tuna Melt 203

Grilled Tofu Spiedini
with Summer Vegetables 204

Risotto Pomodoro 206

Heartbeet Risotto 207

Frittata 211

I DOLCI

Tiramisu 214

Zeppole 216

Sanguinaccio 217

Pignoli Cookies 218

Panna Cotta 221

Almond Macaroons 223

Chocolate Hazelnut Macaroons 225

Affogato 226

Lemon Mint Granita 228

Coffee Granita 229

Sweet Summer Peaches in White Wine .. 231

ACKNOWLEDGMENTS 232

INDEX 234

ABOUT THE AUTHORS 240

MY STORY

SOMETIMES I THINK I WAS DESTINED to become a chef. Cooking for others is in my blood—my Italian blood.

The vegan part came later. That wasn't in my blood. That was in my heart.

I have always loved my family's cooking, and I truly value my Italian heritage. When I first became a vegan, I worried that I might have to sacrifice one or the other, or both. It turns out that I never had to sacrifice anything! The plant-based dishes I created were just as delicious and true to my heritage as the non-plant-based dishes I grew up with. I still love Italian food more than any other type of cuisine, and my plant-based versions of it are, in my opinion, completely authentic. (Fortunately, the guests who come to Pura Vita, my restaurant, all agree!)

I should know: I grew up in a typical Brooklyn and Long Island Italian household where we spent more time cooking than we spent watching television, reading books—and probably anything else. My parents organized our home around food. The kitchen was where they showed us their love. There was so much, it all barely fit inside the house—and they shared their love, and their food, with as many people as possible.

Many of my childhood friends came from broken homes. As a result, they often had no other place to go after school except our house,

(Top) Me at three years old with Grandma and Grandpa. (Bottom) Five-year-old me with Grandpa, my cousin Tracey, Grandma, and my cousin Eric.

where no one ever needed an invitation. All of my friends were always welcome at my parents' front door and greeted with just one question: "What would you like to eat?" and soon enough they were offered a plate of food. Dinner at the Punzone home could be four of us, or fourteen of us. It didn't matter to my parents. The more people at the table, the more cooking they could do, and the more they could share. This was the Brooklyn, the Italian way.

Not surprisingly, both of my parents absolutely loved to cook. And although they could whip up just about anything, my father's specialty was *peppas*, or peppers, and he particularly loved a New York variety called Italian long hots (which, for some reason, you can't buy on the West Coast. I miss them!). My dad cooked the peppas with oil, garlic, and whatever was sitting in our kitchen cabinets, but he always added something crunchy and something sweet, such as nuts and raisins (see page 106 for one of my favorite peppas recipe, one of the specialties at Pura Vita). But what my dad most enjoyed was working with peppers so hot that it became a competition among my friends to see who could actually eat them. Most of them said, no problem. Most of them ended up turning bright red, and not from embarrassment.

My mom favored more traditional, straightforward southern Italian cooking, where everything starts with garlic, olive oil, and tomatoes. Pasta was her specialty, and every Sunday she made "gravy," aka marinara sauce. (I give my take on her sauce on page 37.) One of my favorite memories will always be waking up to the sound of a metal spoon clanging on the pot, a sound that even today takes me back to mornings in my childhood bedroom.

If the heart of our home was the kitchen, the heart of the kitchen was the large table where we spent much of our time eating but also talking, socializing, and anything else that involved getting together. (We weren't allowed in the living room because, as in most Italian households on Long Island, that room was off-limits; and, regardless, the sofa and chairs were all covered with that strange clear plastic that crunched and sighed if you were ever permitted to sit on it.)

My parents were just following in their parents' culinary footsteps. My grandparents on my father's side came over from Italy when they were very young; his mother from Calabria and his father from Gragnano, a small hillside town near Naples that is so synonymous with pasta that in 2013 the European Union designated Gragnano a Protected Geographical Indication. Both grandparents came from enormous families—my grandmother had about twenty siblings, my grandfather just a couple fewer, so I have more than one hundred cousins, most of whom probably consider cooking as important today as it was for my grandparents.

When my grandparents settled in America, they started a small grocery store in the Crown Heights section of Brooklyn. There they worked

(Top left) Both grandmas and me. (Top right) Grandpa and me. (Bottom left) Grandpa, Grandma, and five-year-old me. (Bottom right) Grandpa and me eating birthday cake. (Following page) Daddy as a little boy with Grandpa and Grandma at a Louis Prima concert.

MY GRANDPARENTS, THE PUNZONES

"If you talk to people in that neighborhood, they'll remember Punzone's," said Jerome Krase, the former director of the Center for Italian American Studies at Brooklyn College and a sociologist who has focused on Italian American culture and its people. His wife grew up just two blocks from the deli, and he told me that these businesses were as important as church to Italian immigrants and their children. "Everything is ritualized," Krase said. "Even going to Punzone's for a hero sandwich—it wasn't merely the eating of the food, but the interaction with the owner and the people that were there and the people that you went to get food for."
—Katie Honan, *Bon Appétit*

from five o'clock in the morning until they basically passed out from exhaustion at midnight. Over the years my grandfather became known as the king of the neighborhood; and all kinds of people—from local workers to employees from the sanitation department just down the street—came to the store to savor his famous heroes. Heroes (also called subs, hoagies, grinders, as well as many other names depending on where you live) were the specialty of the house, although the shop also served other standard Italian meals, including eggplant, veal, and artichoke parmigiana.

But it was the heroes that truly made my grandparents famous. Oddly, my grandparents didn't intend to start serving food—but as their grocery store became a place where regulars in the neighborhood would drop by, it slowly evolved into a hero shop as well. It was the family tradition that when people showed up, feeding them was essential.

Everyone knew and loved my grandfather. Naturally, as a child, I decided I wanted to be just like him: someone who provides the entire community with nourishment and happiness. My grandparents made people happy by feeding the body and the soul. I wanted to do the same.

When I would say this to my father, he was supportive in the sense that he believed that I could do whatever I wanted to do in life. But he added a caveat: Please don't open up a restaurant! In his eyes, running a restaurant meant that I wouldn't have time to do anything else. He was wrong and he was right—I do own a restaurant, and, yes, there's barely room for anything else in my life! But I couldn't imagine having it any other way.

❦

That's one side of my cooking story—the importance of food in my life: preparing it, eating it, sharing it, loving it.

The other side of my cooking story is about becoming a vegan.

The process started when I was ten years old. Before that, I had always thought that if you ate a piece of meat, some sweet, doe-eyed cow was generously providing you with that little morsel, and in return she was now missing a small sliver of her body, your dinner.

This wasn't good, but at least the animal was still alive.

Then, when I was in the fifth grade, my teacher showed the entire class a video of a slaughterhouse—which I admit was unusual for a teacher of impressionable ten-year-olds—and I finally realized that butchers weren't just cutting a dainty little hole in the cow's side. They were killing the cows in ways that absolutely horrified me. I just sat in class and cried my eyes out. I couldn't believe that, in reality, we were tearing our teeth into the carcasses of dead animals.

That did it. Right then and there. I went home determined to tell my parents that I would never eat meat again.

Remember: My mom and dad were people for whom enjoying all kinds of food was a prerequisite to happiness, to living a full life. I was petrified to have this conversation. I was telling them I wasn't going to eat animals anymore. For a family for whom all food was enjoyable, this was not an easy task.

This is still one of the most vivid memories of my childhood, sitting on the steps near the kitchen where I could see my parents cooking dinner but being far too frightened to actually go in and tell them my news. What would I say? More frightening: What would they say?

Finally, I walked into the kitchen and sat down.

"I need to talk to you about something I saw today and how it made me feel," I said. Then I told them about the video and my reaction to it. I ended my little speech with, "I want you to know that I'm not going to eat meat anymore."

I studied their faces. They didn't give much away. In fact, for several moments they were totally quiet. I think they were trying to process what this strange little ten-year-old was telling them. They must have thought I was from another planet.

Then they spoke. They were confused, concerned, confounded. My dad also began to make fun of me and my newly found vegetarianism, but that was the way he was—if my dad didn't make fun of you, it meant he didn't like you.

Mostly they seemed to think that I was just going through some kind of strange prepubescent stage and that I would eventually lose interest. After all, our ancestry was one of not just eating meat but making a living from it.

Once my mom had eventually digested all this information, she asked, "Okay, if you won't eat meat, what is it that you want to eat?"

That was, I realized, an excellent question. I hadn't thought about it yet, so I responded, "Well, I'll eat everything else we eat, but just not the meatballs and chicken cutlets."

That was the start of the Punzone family vegetarian experiment. From then on, my mother would make her usual meals for everyone else, but then work to make my portions vegetarian. (The truth is, she had already eliminated red meat from her own diet for health reasons, but she'd kept this quiet from my dad and my brother.)

This vegetarianism continued long enough for my parents to slowly realize that my decision wasn't a phase. It was my life. So in their typical supportive, loving fashion, my parents decided that they all had to learn exactly what being a vegetarian meant, and how, as a family, we could work on it together.

I did try to help my mother with preparing this new food regime, but she made most of our meals as always, and I was left with being a prep cook of sorts, picking up tasks like garlic chopping, potato peeling, or salad making.

Then came the next step.

Many people take years to transition from vegetarian to vegan. For me, it was quick.

When I was twelve years old, I started traveling with my mother into Manhattan, where we would eat at places like Angelica's Kitchen,

(Top) Mom and Dad, 1990. (Bottom) Daddy playing guitar.

one of the first all-vegan restaurants in New York. The food was wonderful, but so was the reading material: All the animal protection groups left their pamphlets by the door, and I gobbled them up. I was that kid who, if I became interested in a new idea, would try to learn as much as possible about it, whether it was music or art or photography or, in this case, animal agriculture. I studied every little pamphlet about dairy and eggs as though I were taking an exam on the subject until I finally decided that I could no longer cause any pain to any animals, any time, in any way. I completely rejected the current food system. I was now officially a vegan.

This was more than thirty-five years ago, when being vegan was still considered pretty weird. And if I didn't know that, my brother, Paulie, who is thirteen years older than me, certainly made it clear. The men in my family express their deep and true love for the rest of us with their joking comments, and so Paulie

never stopped mocking me. At every meal he made sure to get in little digs like, "She's vegan, just give her some lettuce." Or "I can't believe how delicious pigs taste." Or "Do you like eating like a rabbit?" This was, however, his way of loving me. And perhaps of nudging me back to his way of eating.

Then came all the questions that those of us who go vegan have to face on a daily basis: *Are you allowed to have chicken broth? Is bread okay? Can you eat pasta? Fish is fine, right?* I always had to say yes or no, but more importantly, I had to explain that I was actually "allowed" to do anything I wanted to do. I was choosing to avoid eating anything that came from an animal. It wasn't some kind of punishment. It was my decision—one that made me happy.

I became unstoppable. By the next year I was so committed to being vegan that I gave away every one of my prized possessions that contained leather, including my Doc Martens boots and my precious leather motorcycle jacket.

Now my parents were truly confused—they'd say things like, "Your jacket was already made, you're not hurting anyone by wearing it now," but I just couldn't own anything that came from an animal. It hurt me.

It wasn't only my family that gave me (loving but confused) abuse. It came from just about everyone in the neighborhood. But I was determined to carry on—and unfortunately I was doing this all by myself. I had no vegan friends, no vegan relatives, no vegan anyone. I was fourteen before I even met another vegan—Ron, a rather terrifying-looking guy with long, greasy black hair whom I often saw at the metal concerts I attended. However, when we finally started talking, he turned out to be incredibly nice and supportive. But outside of Ron, with all those Italian uncles and aunts and cousins by the dozens, it was constant, if affectionate, abuse.

And there were issues to be resolved: for instance, Easter. Easter lasagna was more than food, it was a spectacular celebration. We always had it for dinner and shared it with as many people as we possibly could. But given all my announcements, my mother let me try making a vegan lasagna. It was embarrassing. I just made the lasagna the way we always did, but without cheese, and then crumbled up some tofu for the cheese layers and hoped for the best. My dad tried to hold his niceness together, but after two bites he just said, "Nope. I'm not eating this."

Eventually, we settled into a routine where we all got along. I was vegan, and the rest of the family ate as they always did.

When I was ready to start thinking about what I wanted to do for a living, I remembered my father's recommendation: Whatever you do, do not open a restaurant! So I took his advice and instead went to college and eventually received a master's degree from the School of Visual Arts. Then I became a photographer and worked in a studio. If I wasn't going to cook, I figured that the best way for me to express myself was visually. However, in order to earn a good living, I had to start shooting weddings. That turned out to be totally soul crushing, attending wedding after wedding, night after night. These affairs are difficult enough for the people in them; having the responsibility of taking all of their photos was absolutely horrific. But looking around at these weddings did help me realize something important: I knew I'd rather be feeding people than photographing them.

I eventually decided to walk away from that career. I moved to Rome, where I focused on my passion for Italian food, knowing that one day I would do what I always knew I would do: create clean vegan dishes and share them with the world.

Since I knew my calling was in America, after about a year I moved back to New York City, where I started searching for a job. Like most things in my life, this didn't happen the usual way. I was listening to the Howard Stern radio show while he was talking about Pure Food and Wine, one of New York's premier fine dining vegan restaurants at the time. His description made it sound incredible, so my best friend suggested we eat there for my upcoming birthday. We did, and it was as good as Howard had said—so good, in fact, that I asked the manager what credentials I would need to work there. We talked for a while; he walked me around the place and brought me into the kitchen to meet the chef. The chef then asked me to come back the next week to do a stage, or a kind of internship. That went so well that before the end of the evening, he offered me a job.

My brother Paulie and me on our Brooklyn house's stoop, with our cousins Eric and Tracey.

> What I learned about vegan Italian food applies to any other cuisine and heritage. Whether you're Mexican, French, Korean, or Nigerian, you can stay true to your roots while creating and preparing the same kind of wonderful, delicious dishes that you grew up with. You don't even have to be vegan to enjoy the new recipes you can make. Pasta is, and always will be, *the most comforting food in the world!*
>
> The most common realization I hear from people who decide to lean in to a plant-based lifestyle is this: Cooking a plant-based meal, whether you do it once a week or every day, doesn't mean limiting yourself. Instead, it means learning about the endless new vegetables, fruits, roots, spices, and herbs that will make your meals fantastic. I promise you, no matter what your diet is, no matter what you've cooked in the past, you are guaranteed to discover new tastes, textures, and seasonings. Explore them all and don't feel intimidated! Food is fun; and when you prepare a healthy, delicious dish you feel proud of, there is no better sensation than sharing that dish with someone you care about.

I ended up staying at Pure Food and Wine for five years, but it took me only eighteen months to become executive chef. I was happy. But life has its own ideas: When my partner took a job in Los Angeles, I eventually agreed to move with him, thinking this would be only a few years' sojourn, after which we'd return to the East Coast and I'd return to a vegan New York City life.

That was thirteen years ago.

In Los Angeles, I was lucky enough to land a job as the culinary director of the city's premier vegan, organic, macrobiotic restaurant at the time. My boss was lovely. I learned a great deal from her. But when the ownership changed, I knew it was time for me to start on what was truly my lifelong aspiration—to re-create in an Italian restaurant what my family home had created for everyone in my neighborhood: a safe, welcoming place for everyone to eat, no matter who you were or where you came from. I still believe that no matter what you're feeling, no matter how you're coping, a generous bowl of pasta is going to make you feel better. It's the philosophy I grew up with and will always hold.

So, I created Pura Vita in West Hollywood—the country's first 100-percent vegan Italian restaurant and wine bar. Two years later, we opened Pura Vita Pizzeria. And not long after that, Pura Vita in Redondo Beach.

I come to work every day not just to help run the restaurant—I also come because it makes me happy to see people eat at Pura Vita. (And despite what my father once told me, he loves Pura Vita as much as I do.) It's a place where everyone can be themselves. A place where the food is delicious and comforting and everyone can feel at home.

I feel similarly about the recipes in this book. I am confident that you will find foods that you love here, and I hope you can share them with friends. Share them with your family. Share them with strangers. Invite people to come and eat. Talk about whatever you want. To me, Italian food is Italian life, and Italian life is at its best warm and comforting and filled with love.

THE ITALIAN VEGAN PANTRY

BALSAMIC GLAZE

Balsamic glaze is a thick, reduced version of balsamic vinegar that you can buy at almost any grocery store.

BALSAMIC VINEGAR

Balsamic vinegar is made from reduced grape must, aged for several years in wooden barrels, and produced in either the province of Modena or Reggio Emilia. This vinegar should be dark and concentrated, and aged at least a few years. The highest quality balsamic vinegar will have the certification D.O.P. (same as the San Marzano tomato), which regulates the region in which the product is produced. Do not skimp out on the balsamic vinegar. It can be pricey but it can make all the difference in many dishes.

D.O.P. SAN MARZANO TOMATOES

D.O.P. stands for *Denominazione di Origine Protetta,* which means "protected designation of origin." San Marzano is regarded as culinary sacred ground, due to its perfect tomato-growing conditions, such as its mineral-rich volcanic soil and abundant water. Tomatoes grown in this region are sweeter and more concentrated in flavor, and they make the very best tomato sauce! The D.O.P. certification guarantees that the canned tomatoes so labeled were grown in the Sarnese-Nocerino district in Campania near Naples.

Don't be fooled by the companies that can tomatoes and call them "D.O.P. San Marzano Style Tomatoes" or "Italian Peeled Tomatoes," because, if you read the fine print on the labels, you will see that the tomatoes were not grown in this region and will not taste as sweet or be as fragrant as the real D.O.P. San Marzano tomatoes.

In most cases, these need to be blended, because D.O.P. tomatoes usually come whole in the can.

EGG REPLACER

You don't need conventional eggs, as many egg substitutes are now on the market. My personal preference is Bob's Red Mill Egg Replacer.

EXTRA-VIRGIN OLIVE OIL

Cold-pressed extra-virgin olive oil is one of the most important ingredients to always keep in your pantry. This type of olive oil is known for its rich flavor and versatility for cooking and making dressings. It also has many health benefits, such as numerous antioxidants and heart-healthy fats. Cold-pressed, organic, extra-virgin olive oil is the least-processed variety and therefore the healthiest type of oil. Most important, its wonderful flavor and aroma are exactly what you will need to make all my recipes taste amazing.

Olive oil (regular, not extra-virgin) is made from a blend of refined olive oils and virgin olive oils. Extra-virgin olive oil is a much higher quality food than regular olive oil.

Olive oil doesn't stay good forever. Once bottled, it has an eighteen- to twenty-four-month shelf life, so you should purchase it within twelve to eighteen months of its harvest date (which is printed on the label) and you should use it up within six months after opening the bottle.

FLOURS

Although all-purpose flour doesn't have much flavor, it's required in many dishes, such as pizzas, focaccias, and other baked goods, and for thickening sauces and dredging food before frying.

Double zero flour, also known as doppio zero, also known as pasta fresca, is a finely ground Italian flour commonly used to make pasta and pizza dough. It's often abbreviated as 00.

Semolina flour is made from ground durum wheat. This flour's high protein and gluten content makes it perfect for making pasta, as these properties help to shape the pasta and maintain its shape when cooked.

FRESH HERBS

Fresh herbs are absolutely essential. Basil, parsley, rosemary, and thyme are the most frequently used in my recipes. You must always have fresh basil and Italian parsley (the flat-leaf kind, not the curly kind) in your fridge, ready to go.

GARLIC

No Italian pantry would be complete without this staple. Nearly every savory recipe contains a bit of garlic (or, if you are anything like me, a lot!).

Consider practicing the best way to peel the garlic. Lay the flat side of the knife blade on a clove of unpeeled garlic. Place the heel of your hand toward the spine of the knife (not on top of the blade) and press down on the knife with your palm to smash the clove, separating it from the skin.

Consider further smashing the clove before you mince or slice! Smashing the peeled clove of garlic breaks more cell walls than slicing, cutting, or mincing the whole clove. Smashing or crushing garlic also creates the maximum amount of allicin, the compound that gives garlic its smell, and releases its most potent flavor.

MALDON FLAKY SEA SALT

Some people might say that salt is salt, but some salt works better than others for different dishes. I often recommend Maldon salt to finish a beautiful dish. Maldon salt has unusual pyramid-shaped, crunchy flakes, and it tends to bring out a clean flavor that enhances any dish in both taste and texture.

NUTRITIONAL YEAST

Nutritional yeast is a deactivated yeast sold in powder or flakes (I prefer the flakes). Often called "nooch" by its fans, it has a cheesy, umami flavor and is essential in many recipes from ricotta to parmigiana.

NUTS (ALMONDS, CASHEWS, PISTACHIOS)

Traditionally, many Italian recipes require nuts, but my versions of Italian recipes require a lot of them! Almonds, cashews, pistachios, and macadamias are the kinds you will see most often in this book. Nuts can be safely stored at room temperature for at least a month; refrigerate them if you will not use them within a month.

I use raw cashews very often, as they're a neutral-tasting nut that adds the perfect amount of fat to make dishes creamy without overwhelming their flavor profiles.

OLIVES

Olives are high in fat, but they make up for this by also being high in vitamin E and many important antioxidants. According to the Cleveland Clinic, olives can also improve your heart health, increase your intake of fiber, help manage your blood sugar levels, and reduce your risk of cancer.

Some of my favorite varieties include Kalamata olives—large, dark brown olives with a smooth, meaty texture. The best Kalamata olives are grown in Greece and are usually preserved in vinegar or olive oil. I use pitted (pits removed) Kalamatas in many of my dishes and pizzas. Stock up on these little salty treasures!

I also love Castelvetrano olives, which have a bright green color and meaty texture, and are buttery, rich, and delectable. Their flavor is mild and both somewhat salty and slightly sweet, making them appealing to those who shy away from the stronger, briny olive varieties.

A few other favorites are Niçoise, Gaeta, and Cerignola olives.

Olives are best when purchased marinated or cured, freshly displayed in the store, or in jars from a reputable brand. They generally stay good for at least a year (but they've never lasted nearly that long in my presence!).

OREGANO

This dried herb is a must for your pantry. It adds lots of flavor, but keep in mind that a little goes a long way. If you can find Sicilian oregano, do not pass up the opportunity to stock up—Sicilian oregano has a unique, wonderful fragrance that is much more intense than any other variety. If you can't find it, regular oregano will always do the job. Rub it between your fingers before adding it to your dish to release the oils.

PANKO

Panko are Japanese bread crumbs made from crustless loaves of bread that are steamed and then processed into flakes and dried. The flakes are larger than standard bread crumbs and tend to keep foods crisper longer. My preferred brand of panko is Edward & Sons Organic.

PASTA DI GRAGNANO

Pasta made in Gragnano is simply the best-quality pasta. The hill town of Gragnano is famous throughout Italy and the world for its exceptional air-dried, bronze-cut pastas. Additionally, Gragnano is where my grandpa came from, so even more of a reason to stay true to my roots!

Pasta di Gragnano can be purchased in any Italian specialty store, or you can order it online (as much as we love local markets, you can often find products online that you might not find in a small town). This pasta comes in every shape and size you can think of; you should try them all to see which is your favorite. Pasta di Gragnano can be slightly more expensive than pasta made in other places, but I believe it is worth tasting some to see if you agree!

It's always a good idea to keep various shapes of pasta in your pantry. Here are some of the ones I like, both long and short. Don't forget the little ones for soup.

For dried pastas, there are seemingly end-less shapes to play with! Some examples are:

LONG
Bucatini, capellini, fettuccine, lasagna, linguine, spaghetti, tagliatelle

SHORT
Campanelle, casarecce, cavatappi, conchiglie, farfalle, fusilli, gemelli, maccheroni, orecchiette, paccheri, penne, radiatori, rigatoni, ziti

SOUP
Acini di pepe, ditalini, orzo, pastina, stelline

PEPERONCINO

No, I am not referring to the pickled and jarred peppers. In southern Italian cooking, chili is an extremely important ingredient. We use this pepper for various dishes or as a topping for just about anything, as long as you can appreci-ate some heat! In Calabria, in the warm summer months especially, you can find thousands of these peperoncino strung together on wires and hung up from buildings left to fry in the hot air. This is truly one of my favorite and most loved visuals in the south of Italy.

You can purchase peperoncino just about anywhere that sells Italian ingredients or online. There are many varieties of peperoncino: whole Calabrian chili peppers and flakes, chili powder, and, most amazingly, Calabrian chili pepper paste (spread/sauce), sometimes called *bomba calabrese* (I put this on almost everything I eat). I also make chili oil by putting chili flakes or ground chili in a glass bottle with extra-virgin olive oil. Shake the bottle and then let it rest for a day or two. This chili oil will enhance all your pasta, pizza, and sandwiches.

POTATOES

Present in many Italian dishes, potatoes are one of the most versatile vegetables you should always have on hand. There are many types of potatoes, but my favorite, and the type I suggest you use in my recipes, is Yukon gold. Its natu-rally smooth, buttery texture makes for delicious baked, roasted, fried, or mashed potatoes.

If you store your potatoes at room tempera-ture, they will last two to three weeks. Don't refrigerate them! They'll spoil quicker; the cold converts the potato's starch into sugar. It's best to store potatoes in a cool and dark place with proper ventilation and little moisture.

RICE

Rice is a staple in a multitude of Italian dishes. Short-grain Arborio and carnaroli rice have a high starch content, perfect for creating the rich and creamy texture of Italian risottos.

Arborio and carnaroli rice can stay fresh for two to three years if stored in airtight containers away from moisture. It is important to properly store your specialty rice, as it can be more expensive than other types of rice.

VEGETABLE STOCK

If you are not planning to make your own vegetable stock, my preferred brand for all my recipes is Imagine's vegetarian No-Chicken Broth, a clear broth made from onions, celery, and carrots. Avoid vegetable stocks that are not clear and might be heavy on the carrots or other sweeter vegetables, as this is not the flavor profile my dishes require.

WINE AND SPIRITS

I could write an entire book about wine and its relationship to Italian food (and someday I might!), but for now I just want to mention some of my favorite wines. I am a firm believer

When I first became a vegan (in the early 1990s), I had a lot of friends whose houses I would often visit, sometimes for parties, sometimes just to hang out. But every time I went, I knew I'd have to eat beforehand because there would never be anything I could eat. If a friend's mom was cooking dinner or preparing snacks for a party, I had to explain to her why I couldn't eat her food, and this was too often misunderstood. Many times, the mother would call up my mother and say, "I think maybe you might want to look into your daughter's eating habits." Or "We suspect your daughter has an eating disorder." Or "You might want to check out if Tara is getting enough nutrition."

My poor mother always stuck up for me and said (more or less), "My daughter is vegan. She's a very healthy eater. But she always eats before she leaves our house."

"Well," the friend's mother might respond, "we could always make her a salad."

My mom would then explain that I didn't want to eat salad all the time, I wanted hearty food. Throwing iceberg lettuce into a bowl with some balsamic vinegar was not a full meal.

Today things are much different, at least in many households. I feel sorry for those who live in places where "vegan" is still considered weird or a disorder. It isn't. It's just a more mindful and healthier lifestyle.

that Italian meals should be complemented with Italian wines and followed by an amaro to help you digest properly.

Sparkling wines are fabulous, especially on a hot summer day. I always enjoy a chilled prosecco or Lambrusco in the warmer weather to go along with the antipasti course.

Vino bianco (white wine): Cortese di Gavi, Pecorino, and Vermentino. These wine varietals are commonly super fresh, with a high level of acidity and herbaceousness. These will complement any of the lighter dishes, such as grilled vegetables, as well as the creamy pasta dishes or even pesto.

Vino rosso (red wine): It's difficult to choose just a few here as frankly I love almost all Italian red wines. But some of my favorites are Nero d'Avola, Nebbiolo, Etna Rosso, and a beautifully balanced Super Tuscan wine. Red wine should always be paired with heavier dishes, such as pastas with tomato sauce or eggplant parmigiana.

Amaro (Italian for "bitter") is a liqueur traditionally made from herbs, spices, and other flavorings. It's consumed after dinner as a digestif. Amari have bittersweet flavors and are served neat at room temperature. You can definitely chill an amaro; that might make it more palatable for a beginner. Amari are indeed a bit strong on the palate and may not be for everyone, but I recommend giving them a try. Some of my favorites are Fernet-Branca, Nonino, and Nocino.

TERMS AND TOOLS

AL DENTE

This is an extremely important term to understand, as it will appear often in this book. Pasta cooked "al dente" means the pasta still has some bite to it when chewed and should still have a small amount of white inside when cut into. This is the texture at which pasta should always be served.

When I mention cooking the pasta for "a little more than half the recommended cooking time" (which will vary greatly depending on the shape and brand of pasta), this indicates the pasta will still be a bit too crunchy when you bite into it. You will then use pasta tongs to transfer the pasta to a sauté pan and finish cooking it there, along with some of the water you cooked it in and the other ingredients in the dish. This makes for the perfect marriage of flavors and textures.

BLANCHING

Blanching is the process by which vegetables are briefly submerged in boiling water and then immediately cooled to stop further cooking, allowing them to maintain their vibrant color and flavor. Drain the blanched vegetable, then shock it by plunging it in a bowl of very cold water or ice water, or running it under cold water. Once the vegetable is thoroughly cold, drain and gently dry it.

CHINOIS

A chinois (pronounced "shin-wa") is a cone-shaped sieve with an extremely fine mesh used to strain stocks, purees, soups, and sauces, producing a very smooth texture. When you need a velvety sauce, you reach for your chinois!

DICING

Dicing means cutting food into small, square, uniformly sized pieces. Dicing allows for distribution of flavor and texture throughout the dish. There are three sizes of dice cuts. Small (or fine) dices are approximately ¼-inch cubes, medium are ½-inch cubes, and large are ¾-inch cubes. Diced foods are quite aesthetically pleasing.

FOOD MILL

I use a food mill, a utensil with a hand-cranked blade that forces food through the holes in a plate, in my recipes primarily to remove tomato skins for fresh tomato sauce.

FOOD PROCESSOR

An electric food processor takes on the tough and rigorous work of shredding, kneading, and grinding, and it can also be used like a blender to combine ingredients into smooth mixtures. A food processor allows you to create dishes using fresh, whole ingredients, including nuts, with silky smooth results.

HIGH-SPEED BLENDER

High-speed blenders are more powerful than regular blenders—the motors have greater horse-power and their blades are sharper. They typically have larger canisters and offer accessories like tampers to help blend tough ingredients. If I had to eliminate all the appliances in my kitchen and keep only one, it would be my high-speed blender. Personally, I swear by my Vitamix. (They are not endorsing me; it's just my truth!)

JULIENNE

Julienne means cutting food, such as carrots or zucchini, into long, thin strips.

MANDOLINE

The mandoline, also called a vegetable slicer, is used to cut firm vegetables or fruits into uniform slices or shapes. Use a mandoline when you need to slice something paper-thin. The mandoline can help you take your prep time down quite a bit. The food is pushed down a slanted surface to a fixed, extremely sharp blade. Be very careful while using a mandoline, even if you are a professional chef—it's all too easy to slice your fingers.

MOKA

A Moka is an Italian stovetop espresso pot that you can find online for as cheap as $6. I bought my first one while I was living in Rome. I had no idea I would never be able to live without this simple little device!

NUT MILK BAG

This is a fabric bag through which you can strain your blended raw nut milk to remove the excess pulp or fiber. The best type of nut milk bag is made from commercial-grade nylon mesh. This will ensure the strongest durability and perfect straining for pulp-free results.

PASTA MACHINE

A pasta machine can elevate your homemade pasta to the next level. There are several different types of pasta machines, some manual, some electric. Both are great and can help you explore your pasta obsession (which you will develop). Don't be tricked by price: More expensive does not always mean better. Stainless steel manual pasta machines are wonderful. I have been using my grandmother's Marcato manual pasta machine for the past twenty-five years—and she had it from God knows when. It still works perfectly.

PASTA WATER

The secret for making incredible pasta dishes is using the water in which you've boiled your pasta. As pasta cooks, it releases starch. This starchy water will help bind the sauce to the pasta—almost like glue!—creating a perfect combination of textures and flavors. For most of my pasta dish recipes, I instruct you to transfer some of the pasta water into your sauté pan to finish cooking your pasta with the other ingredients. I never dump my pasta water down the drain until I am completely done cooking the dish. You never know when you might want some more!

Also, the importance of salting cannot be overstated. Adding enough salt to the pasta water seasons the pasta and contributes to the finished dish. The usual ratio is approximately two to four tablespoons of salt to six quarts of water. When I cook, I never actually measure the salt for pasta water. I just trust my instincts. This is so very important, as tasting for salt and adding it as you are cooking is the key to ensure each dish is properly seasoned to your taste. Once you add salt, you cannot remove it.

POTATO RICER

A potato ricer looks a bit like a large garlic press. It pushes cooked potatoes through tiny holes, making them smooth enough to use for dishes like gnocchi. You will not get the same results using a grater or a food processor. So if you plan to make gnocchi, a potato ricer is necessary.

ROUGH CHOP

To rough chop is to cut something into pieces without concern over the exact size and uniformity. Some recipes may specify for an ingredient to be roughly chopped; the irregularity of size doesn't matter, as it will be blended.

SAUTÉ PAN

A sauté pan is a relatively shallow pan with straight sides (a skillet, or frying pan, has slanted sides). These straight sides make the sauté pan good for cooking ingredients in a liquid, as in shallow frying, braising, or saucing pastas, because these liquids could easily spill over a skillet's slanted sides. You can generally perform the same cooking tasks in either a skillet or a sauté pan, but in a perfect world, you would have one of each.

THE MUSIC OF FOOD

I believe that food brings people together. I am also confident that music does the same. Food has always been a part of my life, but so has music. My father was a professional singer in a doo-wop group, and he was passionate about music. As a result, he was adamant that I learn all about these singers, the groups, the songs, the lyrics, and their meanings. My dad and I listened to music every day—mostly doo-wop from the 1950s (which is the inspiration for what I play most every night in the restaurant). This music takes me back to my childhood in such a strong way, I can almost smell it! It makes me want to start cooking a big pot of sauce!

Of course, there was other music as well, such as old Americanized Italian songs from Lou Monte, Tony Bennett, Louis Prima, and Jimmy Roselli. And then there was the good ol' solid rock and roll. I doubt there was a single day that my father wasn't listening to singers like Little Richard, Fats Domino, Chuck Berry, and Bo Diddley. I can't get enough of this kind of music still to this day.

Around the time I turned ten, I also started listening to heavy metal, punk, goth, and other music my father never understood. It was heavy. It was aggressive. It motivated me. And the most interesting new connection with this type of music was the veganism within the scene. I was a part of a movement. Things were changing. Here were many people who fighting for animal rights. I was there for it!

Today, when I cook, music must be playing. It's the soul of everything I do. Listening to music gives me spirit. It gives me energy. It brings out the best in me. It makes me want to keep going. Food is my love language. Music is my therapy.

THE
BASICS

RICOTTA

Ricotta, one of the world's most popular cheeses, is a necessity when it comes to Italian cuisine. This recipe is one of many examples of my mimicking a traditional style of cheese to make it vegan. Keep in mind that it's important to make your ricotta light, airy, and easily spreadable, which will allow it to be used in many different recipes in many different applications.

I have two versions: a cashew-based and an almond-based ricotta. The cashew ricotta heats up really well and is therefore excellent in dishes, such as lasagnas, that are baked and served hot. The almond ricotta is much lighter and works better in salads and on cheese plates. Despite their differences, both ricottas should be light, tangy, and able to go with everything—because that's what ricotta cheese is: something that can go with just about anything you want it to go with.

These cheeses mean a great deal to me. Sundays at my childhood home always meant pasta. Before I went vegan, my mom cooked up an accompanying meat sauce, but to accommodate my new lifestyle, she started making marinara sauce instead, which bothered my brother, Paulie, as it meant no more meatballs, no pork, no braciola—in fact, none of the meats that he loves. But there was still a bowl of fresh ricotta, along with the broccoli rabe and pasta.

After I went vegan, one of the most important items on my to-do list was to create a ricotta without any animal products. I tried it over and over until, when I was twenty, I finally got the cheese exactly right. How did I know this version worked? Paulie, who makes fun of me more than anyone else in the world, and who would feel uncomfortable if he didn't hold that title, ate some with the sole intention of tearing me to shreds. His reaction was unlike any other I've ever seen from him: he took a bite, then another, then another, and finally said, "That's actually really good." And then he put a big spoonful of it on his pasta.

CASHEW RICOTTA

MAKES APPROXIMATELY 9 CUPS

(Enough for a full tray of lasagna or parmigiana di melanzane)

Raw cashews are interesting; they don't have much taste on their own, meaning you can make them taste however you want them to taste. But they have just the right amount of fat to create these creamy types of dishes.

1 quart raw, unsalted cashews

2 cups extra-virgin olive oil

1 cup filtered water

¼ cup minced garlic

½ cup apple cider vinegar

¼ cup nutritional yeast

2 tablespoons sea salt

1 tablespoon black pepper

2 pounds super firm tofu

1 Soak the cashews in water for a minimum of 4 hours. Drain and rinse well.

2 Place the cashews, olive oil, water, garlic, vinegar, yeast, salt, pepper, and tofu in a high-speed blender and blend until smooth.

3 Store in an airtight container in the refrigerator for up to 5 days.

TIP: If you cannot find super firm tofu, you can use firm instead. Make sure to squeeze all the excess water from the firm tofu. The texture of the ricotta will be slightly less dense but the taste will remain the same.

ALMOND RICOTTA

MAKES APPROXIMATELY 6 CUPS

1 Soak the blanched almonds in water for a minimum of 1 hour. Drain and rinse the almonds well.

2 Place the lemon juice, olive oil, vinegar, yeast, and salt in the jar of a high-speed blender. Add the almonds and water, then blend until smooth.

3 Store in an airtight container in the refrigerator for up to 5 days.

3½ cups sliced blanched almonds

½ cup lemon juice

½ cup extra-virgin olive oil

2 tablespoons apple cider vinegar

2 tablespoons nutritional yeast

2 teaspoons sea salt

½ cup filtered water

CASHEW MOZZARELLA

MAKES APPROXIMATELY 7 CUPS

Mozzarella is one of the most popular cheeses in America—and in Italy as well. Mozzarella should always be light in flavor and texture. Unfortunately, many of the vegan mozzarella options on the market are too thick, heavy, and not particularly meltable. So my goal for vegan mozzarella was to make it light with a wonderful texture that can complement any dish.

Mozzarella is excellent just by itself or in a caprese salad.

2 cups raw, unsalted cashews

1 quart filtered water

¼ cup nutritional yeast

2 tablespoons, plus 2 teaspoons apple cider vinegar

2 tablespoons sea salt

2 teaspoons garlic powder

2 tablespoons refined coconut oil

½ cup tapioca starch

TIP: You should adjust the amount of tapioca you use depending on which dish you plan to use the mozzarella in. For example, if you plan to use the mozzarella melted or soft, use about ¼ cup tapioca. If you plan to make a caprese salad, you will want the cheese to be firmer.

1 Soak the cashews in water for a minimum of 4 hours. Drain and rinse well before using.

2 Add the cashews, water, yeast, vinegar, salt, garlic powder, and coconut oil to the jar of a blender or food processor. Blend until smooth.

3 Pour the mixture into a saucepan.

4 Stir in the tapioca. Cook over low heat, stirring until completely combined. Reduce the heat so the cheese is at a low boil and cook for 8 to 10 minutes. The cheese should have a very thick consistency (you should have a hard time stirring it).

5 Remove from the heat and let cool.

6 Store in an airtight container in the refrigerator for up to 5 days.

MACADAMIA PARMIGIANO

MAKES 2 CUPS

Parmigiano is another cheese that Italians seem to use on nearly everything. This Macadamia Parmigiano is very simple to make, composed of just macadamia nuts and nutritional yeast (with a little pinch of salt).

1 cup raw, unsalted macadamia nuts

1 cup nutritional yeast

1 teaspoon sea salt

TIP: Yes, macadamia nuts are expensive, but they do work the best to make vegan parmigiano—and you don't need that many. But you can use cashews, almonds, walnuts, Brazil nuts, and even pumpkin seeds instead.

---

1   Place the macadamia nuts, yeast, and salt in the jar of a high-speed blender or food processor. Pulse until the mixture has the consistency of a fine crumble. Do not overprocess into a paste or butter.

2   Store in an airtight container.

TIP: Make sure your blender is 100 percent dry before adding the ingredients!

MARINARA SAUCE

MAKES APPROXIMATELY 11 CUPS

Perhaps the most important day in an Italian American household is the one on which your mother makes the marinara sauce.

Every Sunday my mother and my grandmother would wake up early in the morning and start the process, tending it for hours upon hours. That wonderful smell would then seep throughout the whole house. It was such a beautiful aroma, so peaceful and relaxing, because it made you realize it was Sunday and you were going to have all day with your family; and, best of all, you knew you were going to eat really well. The day was going to be all about food and laughing and maybe some arguing and whatever else but above all, family. There's something about the sauce that just brought everybody together.

Throughout the day, as the sauce was simmering, one by one each member of my family would rip off large pieces of bread and stick them into the giant pot of sauce. My mother would scream, "Ah, get out of here. What are you doing? Get yourself a little bowl. Don't do that. That's disgusting. *Schifo!* Stop it."

We didn't care. Me and my brother, we could eat a whole loaf of Italian bread, just dipping it in the giant vat of sauce. When my brother had children, his son Anthony picked up the habit—he's been known to stick an entire loaf of bread in the pot of sauce.

Learning how to make a good pot of sauce is one of the most important tasks in Italian cooking. So let's make marinara.

¼ cup extra-virgin olive oil

1 cup finely diced onion

¼ cup minced or sliced (super thin) garlic

¼ teaspoon red chili flakes (optional)

Three 28-ounce cans San Marzano tomatoes (La Valle or La Regina are my favorite brands)

½ cup chopped fresh basil leaves

½ teaspoon black pepper

2 teaspoons sea salt

Growing up in New York, like many Italian Americans, we called red sauce "gravy," no matter how many people scoffed at the word. But when I went to Italy and referred to the sauce as gravy, I got schooled hard. "That's obscene!" they said. I immediately stopped.

1   In a large stockpot, heat the olive oil over medium heat. Sauté the onion, garlic, and red chili flakes, if using, for 8 to 10 minutes, or until the onion is translucent.

2   Add the tomatoes, breaking them up with a spoon. Simmer for 1 hour over low heat, stirring every 10 minutes.

3   Remove from the heat and stir in the basil, pepper, and salt.

4   Store in an airtight container, preferably glass, for up to one week.

CLASSIC PESTO

MAKES APPROXIMATELY 3 CUPS

When I realized—as a kid!—that all I had to change was one single ingredient (using nutritional yeast in place of cheese) to make pesto vegan, I was amazed. This pesto can go on top of any pasta shape, smother your vegetables, or be spread on panini—pretty much any dish you can think of will be enhanced with pesto.

4 cups basil leaves packed

1 cup extra-virgin olive oil

½ cup sliced or slivered blanched almonds

2 or 3 medium to large garlic cloves, to equal 1 tablespoon minced garlic

1 tablespoon nutritional yeast

2 teaspoons lemon juice

1 teaspoon sea salt

½ teaspoon black pepper

¼ teaspoon red chili flakes

1   Place the basil leaves, olive oil, almonds, garlic, yeast, lemon juice, salt, pepper, and chili flakes in the jar of a high-speed blender and blend until combined.

2   Store in an airtight container in the refrigerator.

TIP: Save the pesto in a jar so you always have some on hand.

PESTO CALABRESE

MAKES APPROXIMATELY 3 CUPS

My grandmother comes from Calabria, which is the southernmost mainland region of Italy—the so-called tip of the boot and, in my opinion, where some of the world's best food originates. I was fortunate to be able to learn her magic, as her cooking style differed from the others in my family, who come from the Naples region.

In Calabria everything is just a bit spicier, so when they prepare a pesto, it's a pesto calabrese, made with Calabrian chili peppers and a touch of sun-dried tomato instead of the traditional basil, garlic, and parmigiano. The spice is present but not overwhelming.

2 pounds red bell peppers

¼ cup, plus ½ cup extra-virgin olive oil

1 tablespoon minced garlic

3 tablespoons minced shallot

2 tablespoons sun-dried tomatoes in olive oil, drained

1 cup Almond Ricotta (page 33)

1 tablespoon apple cider vinegar

2 teaspoons sea salt

1 teaspoon black pepper

2 tablespoons Roasted Garlic (page 46)

2 tablespoons whole Calabrian chilis in oil, stems removed

2 tablespoons oil from Calabrian chilis

1　Roast the bell peppers over a grill or burner flame until completely blackened.

2　Place the grilled peppers in a bowl and cover tightly with plastic wrap. Allow them to cool for 15 minutes, and then remove them and peel off the skins. Cut off the stems and remove the seeds.

3　In a sauté pan, heat the olive oil over low heat. Sauté the garlic, shallot, and sun-dried tomatoes for 5 minutes. Remove from the heat and cool.

4　Place the roasted peppers, ¼ cup of the olive oil, garlic, shallot, tomatoes, ricotta, vinegar, salt, pepper, roasted garlic, chilis, and chili oil in a food processor and process until smooth.

5　Pour in the remaining ½ cup of olive oil while the machine is running to emulsify the pesto.

TIP: Save some pesto in a jar so you always have it on hand. Use it for raw vegetable crudités or to spread on grilled ciabatta or panini and, of course, for Calabrese pasta (page 168).

PISTACHIO PESTO

MAKES APPROXIMATELY 3 CUPS

Pistachio pesto is a staple in Sicily. You can use this style of pesto for virtually anything you would use a classic pesto for, but the flavor of the pistachio will give the dish an intense earthy flavor.

---

1   In a high-speed blender, blend the basil, pistachios, garlic, yeast, lemon juice, salt, pepper, chili flakes, and water until nearly smooth.

2   While the machine is running, pour in the olive oil and pistachio oil to emulsify.

3   Store in an airtight container in the refrigerator for up to 5 days.

TIP: Save the pistachio pesto in a jar so you always have it on hand. Use it on raw vegetable crudités or spread on grilled ciabatta or panini and, of course, for pesto pasta in place of the classic pesto (see Pesto Cavatelli, page 167)!

4 cups packed fresh basil leaves

1 cup roasted unsalted pistachios

1 tablespoon minced garlic

1 tablespoon nutritional yeast

2 teaspoons lemon juice

2 teaspoons sea salt

1 teaspoon black pepper

¼ teaspoon red chili flakes

½ cup cold filtered water

½ cup extra-virgin olive oil

½ cup pistachio oil
(La Tourangelle is my favorite)

ROASTED PISTACHIO CRUMBLE

MAKES APPROXIMATELY 2 CUPS

In Sicilian cuisine, pistachios are so valued they have earned the nickname "green gold."

    This roasted pistachio crumble is an excellent addition to almost any roasted or grilled vegetable dish as well as the Heirloom Tomato and Watermelon Salad (page 100). You can buy roasted and salted pistachios from the store or follow this recipe.

2 cups shelled pistachios

1 teaspoon sea salt

---

1   Preheat the oven to 350°F.

2   Place the pistachios in a ziplock bag and smash them to smithereens. You can use a hammer, mallet, or whatever tool you can handle. Be careful not to tear the plastic bag.

3   Pour the smashed pistachios into a mixing bowl and toss in the salt.

4   Spread out on a baking sheet and roast for approximately 5 to 6 minutes, until toasted.

5   Store in an airtight container for up to 2 weeks.

HOW HOWARD STERN JUMP-STARTED MY RESTAURANT CAREER

Once I received my master's degree from the School of Visual Arts, I began a career as a photographer. After all, my father had implored me never to open my own restaurant.

I adore my dad and I do listen to everything he says—but I just couldn't get cooking out of my head. I wanted to share my experience of vegan food with friends, with strangers, with anyone and everyone. Even while I was a photographer, I was doing just that by providing private cooking lessons in people's homes, teaching them how to prepare a whole-foods plant-based diet.

Meanwhile, I loved listening to radio personality Howard Stern, a man whom some love and some hate (me, I love him). One day Howard was talking about a wonderful restaurant, Pure Food and Wine, where he had had an amazing meal.

I hadn't heard of this place and was both amazed and thrilled when I found out the restaurant was vegan (actually, raw vegan)—one of the first of its kind in a fine dining setting. Because of Howard's strong recommendation, I went to Pure Food and Wine the following weekend.

The concept of right place, right time never held truer than it did on that particular night. The moment I arrived I could sense the restaurant was a special place, a place I wanted very much to be a part of, so I asked the general manager what credentials were necessary to work in his kitchen. He didn't know the answer, but he was kind, so he said he'd ask the chef. When he returned from the kitchen, he told me he was going to introduce me to Chef Neal Harden so I could talk to him myself.

This all took place during a busy Saturday evening—I couldn't believe they were taking this time out of their night to even entertain the thought of talking to me. But they did. Chef Neal turned out to be absolutely wonderful, and he politely asked me a couple of questions. He was too busy to engage for more than a few minutes, so he suggested I return the following Tuesday and do a stage with him—which basically meant I would follow him around, watch him work, see how the kitchen operates, and talk to him some more.

I agreed as fast as I could.

That next Tuesday I met with Chef Neal, did the stage, and had the absolute time of my life. Before the night was over, he hired me as a line cook (in a nutshell, a kitchen staff member who prepares the dishes).

There I was, with no experience in a professional commercial kitchen with my foot in the door of a prestigious, fine dining restaurant in Manhattan. I fell instantly in love with my new career and still, to this day, feel very, very grateful to Howard Stern. Without him, this would not have happened.

I ended up working at Pure Food and Wine for a little more than five years. Outside of Pura Vita, it was my favorite job—just an exquisite experience. The other staff members were an incredible group of people who were passionate about food and what they were creating. It was just a beautiful point in time where we were all on the same, happy, fulfilling page and it'll never be matched again.

Along the way I became quite close with Chef Neal, who went on to become the executive chef of abcV, one of restaurateur Jean-Georges Vongerichten's places in Manhattan. Chef Neal taught me so much about how to manage a kitchen; in fact, when I told him I was thinking of attending culinary school, he told me not to, because, he said, I could be teaching the classes myself. That was truly one of the loveliest compliments I've ever received.

Chef Neal was a mentor beyond any mentor I could possibly imagine. He allowed me to work almost every position in the kitchen until I eventually became his sous-chef. I owe much of my success and professional career to that man.

But it was because of Howard Stern that all this started!

ALFREDO SAUCE

MAKES APPROXIMATELY 7 CUPS

Pasta Alfredo, supposedly invented in Rome in 1908, is one of the most popular dishes at Pura Vita, but it's actually not something I grew up with. However, my mother did make us macaroni with parmigiano and butter.

When Pura Vita opened, there was an immediate demand for pasta Alfredo, so I decided to try a version based on my mother's simple butter and cheese recipe, keeping it very light. This Alfredo sauce is quite easy to make and requires few ingredients. You can throw in any vegetable you want, such as asparagus or squash, or any seasonal delight—and it makes for an excellent pasta dish.

4 cups raw, unsalted cashews

2 cups filtered water

½ cup lemon juice

3 tablespoons nutritional yeast

1 tablespoon minced garlic

1 tablespoon sea salt

1 teaspoon black pepper

½ cup extra-virgin olive oil

1   Soak the cashews in water for a minimum of 4 hours. Drain and rinse well before using.

2   Place the cashews, water, lemon juice, yeast, garlic, salt, and pepper in a high-speed blender and blend on medium-high until smooth.

3   With the machine running on low, pour in the olive oil to emulsify.

4   Store in an airtight container for up to 5 days.

TIP: Save some Alfredo sauce in a jar so you always have it on hand to use on raw vegetable crudités or spread on grilled ciabatta or panini, and, of course, for your fettuccine Alfredo.

GREMOLATA

MAKES APPROXIMATELY 5 CUPS

A famous condiment in Italy, gremolata is a pesto-like sauce made with parsley, olive oil, lemon zest, and garlic. I like to punch it up a bit by adding fresh mint and shallots. It should be bright and citrusy. I particularly love it with anything grilled.

---

1 Place the parsley, mint, shallots, garlic, oregano, agave syrup, olive oil, vinegar, lemon juice and zest, salt, pepper, and crushed red pepper in a high-speed blender.

2 Pulse for approximately 1 minute. Do not overblend. The end result should be thick and textured.

3 Store in an airtight container for up to 5 days.

TIP: If you have a mortar and pestle, feel free to use in place of a blender.

4 cups packed fresh parsley leaves

¼ cup fresh mint leaves

2 tablespoons chopped shallots

1½ teaspoons minced garlic

2 tablespoons fresh oregano leaves

1 tablespoon agave syrup

½ cup extra-virgin olive oil

2 tablespoons apple cider vinegar

¼ cup lemon juice

1 tablespoon lemon zest

½ teaspoon sea salt

½ teaspoon black pepper

¼ teaspoon crushed red pepper flakes

ROASTED GARLIC

You cannot move on with your life if you have never enjoyed roasted garlic. Stop immediately, make some, and you will soon understand. Here are two simple ways to make roasted garlic.

WHOLE GARLIC VARIATION

4 garlic bulbs (or as many as you think you will want, which will be more than you anticipate!)

4 tablespoons extra-virgin olive oil

Pinch of sea salt

PEELED GARLIC VARIATION

2 cups peeled garlic cloves

¼ cup extra-virgin olive oil

2 teaspoons sea salt

WHOLE GARLIC VARIATION

1   Preheat the oven to 350°F.

2   Slice approximately ¼ inch off the tops of the garlic bulbs.

3   Place the garlic bulbs, cut side up, on a long sheet of aluminum foil.

4   Drizzle the garlic with olive oil and sprinkle with the salt.

5   Fold the foil over the garlic to make a packet. Place the garlic packet on a small baking sheet. Roast for approximately 45 minutes, or until the bulbs are golden brown and soft.

6   Remove from the oven and cool.

7   Squeeze the garlic from the skins and you're ready to go!

PEELED GARLIC VARIATION

1   Preheat the oven to 350°F.

2   Toss the garlic with the olive oil and salt.

3   Place the garlic on a long sheet of aluminum foil, then fold it over the garlic to form a packet.

4   Put the packet on a baking sheet and roast for 25 to 30 minutes, until the bulbs are golden brown and soft.

5   Remove from the oven and cool.

NOTE: The whole garlic bulbs should be served immediately. The peeled garlic variation can be refrigerated in an airtight container for up to 3 days.

ROASTED GARLIC AIOLI

MAKES APPROXIMATELY 3 CUPS

Roasted garlic aioli is like a fancy Italian-style mayonnaise that you can use on pizzas, paninis, or as a dip for potatoes or any vegetables. It can go on so many different things that you absolutely need to have it ready in your refrigerator at all times!

2 cups raw, unsalted cashews

1 teaspoon lemon juice

1 tablespoon apple cider vinegar

1½ teaspoons sea salt

1 teaspoon nutritional yeast

½ teaspoon Dijon or stone-ground mustard

½ cup cold filtered water

¼ cup Roasted Garlic (page 46)

½ cup extra-virgin olive oil

1   Soak the cashews in water for a minimum of 4 hours. Drain and rinse well before using.

2   Add the cashews, lemon juice, vinegar, salt, yeast, mustard, water, and roasted garlic to the jar of a high-speed blender. Blend until smooth.

3   While the blender is running at low speed, pour in the olive oil to emulsify.

4   The aioli will keep for 6 days in a sealed container in the fridge. You can also freeze it.

CANNELLINI BEANS

MAKES 12 CUPS

Southern Italians use beans very often in their dishes. Learning to soak and cook dry beans is very much worth your time, as they taste better, cost less, and contain a lot less sodium than canned beans.

Soak the beans the night before! You'll need to do this step at least 8 hours before you plan to cook the beans. It can sometimes be a bit of a pain to plan that far ahead, but it's worth it—soaking the beans will shorten their cooking time and make them easier to digest.

4 cups dry cannellini beans

2 teaspoons sea salt

1   Place the beans in a large bowl and sift through them, discarding any stones or debris.

2   Cover the beans with cold water, cover the bowl, and set the beans aside to soak.

3   Drain and rinse the beans. Place them in a large pot and cover them with water, 2 inches above the bean level.

4   Bring the water to a boil and skim off any foam that rises to the top. Reduce the heat and simmer for 30 minutes. Add the salt.

5   Continue simmering for up to 2 more hours, until the beans are tender, checking them every 30 minutes. Add more water as necessary to keep the beans submerged.

6   Do not stir the beans. Simply hold the pot by both handles and swirl the beans around inside the pot. Stirring the beans will end up breaking them into pieces once they are soft. My grandmother would get very upset if she saw you breaking the beans!

7   Store in an airtight container in the refrigerator for up to 5 days.

PANGRATTATO
ITALIAN TOASTED BREAD CRUMBS

MAKES APPROXIMATELY 2 CUPS

Pangrattato, which translates to "grated bread," is my favorite condiment to take my dishes to the next level. It brings texture and crunch to pastas and vegetables. Serve on top of all your favorite dishes!

You can also change up your Pangrattato by adding a pinch of nutritional yeast or even lemon zest, depending on your taste.

4 cups cubed stale ciabatta, sourdough, or gluten-free bread

¼ cup extra-virgin olive oil

2 large garlic cloves

1 tablespoon finely chopped fresh parsley

1 teaspoon black pepper

Pinch of sea salt

1 Place the bread in a high-speed blender or food processor and pulse until you have crumbs.

2 Add the olive oil and garlic to a sauté pan. Cook over very low heat to infuse the garlic into the oil, about 5 minutes.

3 Add the bread crumbs, parsley, pepper, and salt to the pan.

4 Stir constantly until the bread crumbs are golden brown and crispy. Watch carefully so you do not burn the bread crumbs—this can happen very quickly!

5 Remove the garlic. Let the bread crumbs cool before using.

6 Alternatively, you can toast the bread crumb mixture in a 350°F oven for 10 to 12 minutes on a baking sheet, or until golden brown. These can be made ahead of time and stored in an airtight container for up to a week.

CHILI OIL

OLIO SANTO, "HOLY OIL"

MAKES APPROXIMATELY 4 CUPS

I'm telling you right now, homemade chili oil is the most important condiment to have on your table at all times: breakfast, lunch, and dinner. And it is the easiest thing in the world to make.

I personally like to use peperoncino, a dried Italian chili pepper. You just put them in the blender, which breaks up the skin and the seeds and releases the spice in a way that doesn't occur if the seeds aren't broken. If you can't find whole chilis, you could use cayenne or crushed red chili flakes. Chili oil complements just about any and every dish—as long as you like a little heat.

I use this oil for almost everything (except ice cream, and maybe I'll find a way to do that someday).

½ cup peperoncino
(red chili flakes)

3½ cups extra-virgin olive oil
(best quality you can find)

---

1 Make sure the blender is 100 percent dry before adding the chili flakes. Put the peperoncino in the blender and pulverize.

2 Pour the olive oil into a 1-quart glass mason jar (or any glass jar with a lid).

3 Add the pulverized chilis to the oil.

4 Put on the lid and make sure it's on tight.

5 Turn the jar upside down and right side up, making sure all the chili moves from top to bottom and back. Do this every day for 3 to 4 days and the chili will turn the oil red hot! This will stay good at room temperature for up to a year.

GRILLED CIABATTA GARLIC BREAD

SERVES 4 TO 6

There are few things more satisfying than a good piece of grilled ciabatta. Many people like to toast it in the oven, but I prefer to grill the bread, as there's something about those char marks that takes it up to the next level.

Use the best quality ciabatta bread from your local bakery.

½ cup extra-virgin olive oil

2 teaspoons minced fresh garlic

Pinch of sea salt

Tiny pinch of black pepper

Chili flakes (optional)

Loaf of ciabatta

1. In a medium bowl, mix together the olive oil, garlic, salt, pepper, and chili flakes, if using.

2. Preheat the grill. For best results, grill the bread over an open flame.

3. Cut the bread into ½-inch-thick slices.

4. Dip a brush into the oil mixture, making sure to stir all the ingredients well.

5. Brush both sides of the bread lightly with the oil mixture (or heavily depending on your desired taste).

6. Grill each side of the bread over the grill flame until there are visible grill marks on the bread.

7. Serve immediately.

GARLIC CROUTONS

MAKES APPROXIMATELY 2 CUPS

These crunchy, savory croutons can be used in nearly every salad in this book or any other. Day-old bread will work just fine.

¼ cup extra-virgin olive oil

1 teaspoon minced garlic

½ teaspoon sea salt

½ teaspoon black pepper

½ teaspoon nutritional yeast

2 cups ciabatta cubes (roughly ½ to ¾ inch)

1   Preheat the oven to 350°F.

2   Combine the olive oil, garlic, salt, pepper, and yeast in a mixing bowl.

3   Toss the bread cubes in the oil mixture.

4   Spread the bread cubes on a baking sheet and bake for 10 minutes total, flipping halfway.

5   Let cool. Store in an airtight container for up to 3 days.

CASHEW CREAM

MAKES APPROXIMATELY 8 CUPS

Cashew cream is the simplest way to make any vegan dish creamy; it will be a regular in your fridge. You can even use it in coffee instead of the store-bought chemical-filled alternatives.

4 cups raw, unsalted cashews

4 cups filtered water

¼ teaspoon sea salt

1   Soak the cashews in water for a minimum of 4 hours. Drain and rinse them well.

2   Blend the cashews, water, and salt in a blender on high speed until completely smooth. Strain through a chinois or a nut milk bag if you have one, otherwise use as is!

3   Store in the refrigerator for up to 5 days.

SPICED PEPITAS

MAKES 2 CUPS

Pepitas are extremely nutritious and packed with powerful antioxidants. These are an excellent addition to salads and roasted vegetable dishes.

2 cups shelled, raw, unsalted pumpkin seeds

2 teaspoons extra-virgin olive oil

1 teaspoon maple syrup

1 teaspoon sea salt

¼ teaspoon black pepper

¼ teaspoon cayenne

1   Preheat the oven to 350°F.

2   In a medium mixing bowl, combine the pumpkin seeds, olive oil, maple syrup, salt, pepper, and cayenne.

3   Spread the pumpkin seeds on a medium baking sheet and roast for 10 minutes.

4   Remove from the oven, let cool, and store in an airtight container for up to 2 weeks.

I must stress the importance of these basics, as these essential recipes are the building blocks for multiple dishes in this book. Many of these are the finishing touches that will elevate the experience exponentially through taste and texture. These basics can be kept ready to use at any time for any dish. Prepare them and have them ready to use at your fingertips. They are versatile and they are crucial to satisfy your taste buds—and impress your friends and family.

ANTIPASTI

Sicilian Tuna Crostini, *Page 83*

BAKED RICOTTA
Served with GRILLED CIABATTA

SERVES 4 TO 6

Baked ricotta is one of the best-selling dishes on the Pura Vita menu. After you make the Cashew Ricotta (page 33), make Grilled Ciabatta (page 54).

2 cups Cashew Ricotta (page 33)

Extra-virgin olive oil for drizzling

1 tablespoon chopped fresh parsley

Grilled Ciabatta Garlic Bread (page 54)

1 Preheat the oven to 375°F.

2 Place the cashew ricotta in a small (preferably round) baking pan and heat in the oven for 7 to 8 minutes.

3 Drizzle the ricotta with olive oil and top with the parsley.

4 Arrange the ciabatta slices on a serving plate.

TIP: This looks especially delicious when you serve the round baking pan full of bubbling hot cashew ricotta in the center of a platter with the grilled ciabatta displayed all around it. It will not last long.

When I was a kid there were always many people at our dinner table, and my parents served an antipasti course to satisfy them all. The antipasti varied depending on the day and the occasion, but these platters were one of my preferred parts of any meal, because they were a fabulous spread of all kinds of different little snacky items that you could decide how much of which you wanted to eat. A few items were always included: ciabatta, olives, olive tapenade, roasted red peppers, and sometimes carciofi, or little marinated artichokes. This meant there were always plenty of vegan treats. Of course, there was also a separate plate filled with cured meats, but I just ignored that part.

MARINATED OLIVES

MAKES 1 QUART

Occasionally people have told me they don't like olives, and then I question our friendship. Olives are such salty little delights that can liven up so many dishes, from vegetables to pastas to pizzas. But above all, when you're putting together a good antipasti spread, you have to have marinated olives. They're simple to make, and everybody (except the olive haters) will appreciate the time you took to make them from scratch, instead of serving them out of a store-bought jar. The addition of the orange zest makes these olives really pop.

1 to 2 oranges

1 quart fresh unseasoned, unpitted Italian olives (my favorite is Castelvetrano)

¼ cup extra-virgin olive oil

1 sprig rosemary

2 sprigs thyme

1   Zest an orange or two, depending on the size of the fruit, being careful not to include any of the bitter white pith. You want to end up with 2 teaspoons of zest.

2   In a large bowl, combine the orange zest, olives, olive oil, rosemary, and thyme. Mix them well and allow them to marinate at room temperature for at least 2 to 3 hours. Remove the herbs before serving.

3   Serve at room temperature or store in an airtight container in the refrigerator for up to one week.

OLIVE TAPENADE

MAKES APPROXIMATELY 2 CUPS

Olive tapenade is another delicious little treat that you'll find on a cheese plate or on any antipasti board. There are many ways to make olive tapenade, but I prefer these two recipes, with some capers mixed in with lots of parsley and olive oil. You can also prepare the tapenade in a blender, pulsed, or use a mortar and pestle.

2 cups pitted Riviera olives (Taggiasca or Leccino)

1 cup pitted Kalamata olives

¼ cup Roasted Garlic (page 46)

2 tablespoons capers in brine, drained

2 tablespoons lemon juice

1 tablespoon extra-virgin olive oil

¼ cup chopped fresh parsley

½ teaspoon black pepper

Sea salt to taste

1   Pulse the olives, garlic, capers, lemon juice, olive oil, parsley, pepper, and salt in a food processor for a few seconds, until mixed well. It should be chunky rather than totally smooth.

2   Refrigerate in an airtight container for up to one week.

CASTELVETRANO OLIVE TAPENADE

MAKES APPROXIMATELY 3 CUPS

Many different kinds of olives will work here, although my favorites are buttery, delicious Castelvetrano olives.

2 cups pitted Castelvetrano olives

1 tablespoon minced garlic

2 tablespoons chopped fresh parsley

2 tablespoons capers in brine, drained

1 teaspoon fresh thyme leaves

1 teaspoon fresh oregano leaves

1 teaspoon lemon zest

1 teaspoon orange zest

1 teaspoon sea salt, plus more as needed

½ teaspoon black pepper

2 tablespoons extra-virgin olive oil

1   Pulse the olives, garlic, parsley, capers, thyme, oregano, lemon and orange zests, salt, pepper, and olive oil in a food processor for a few seconds until mixed well. The mixture should be chunky rather than totally smooth. Taste for salt.

2   Refrigerate in an airtight container for up to one week.

BRUSCHETTA

SERVES 2 TO 4

Bruschetta in Italian is pronounced broo-SKETT-tah. Traditionally, this is toasted bread rubbed with fresh garlic and topped with fresh ripe tomatoes, plenty of good olive oil, and a pinch of salt.

8 slices of ciabatta or sourdough bread

½ cup, plus ¼ cup extra-virgin olive oil

2 teaspoons minced garlic

2 pinches of sea salt, plus more as needed

Tiny pinch of black pepper

Pinch of chili flakes (optional)

2 cups cherry or grape tomatoes, cut into quarters

2 garlic cloves, smashed

4 basil leaves, torn into very small pieces

1   In a medium bowl, combine ½ cup of the olive oil, the minced garlic, a pinch of salt, pepper, and chili flakes, if using.

2   Brush one side of a bread slice lightly with the oil mixture (or heavily, depending on your desired taste).

3   Place the bread in a toaster oven (set on toast) or broil in a regular oven until golden brown. If you use the stove broiler, do not walk too far away—it only takes a minute or two before the toast will burn!

4   In a separate bowl, combine the quartered tomatoes, remaining ¼ cup of olive oil, the smashed garlic, basil leaves, and another pinch of salt.

5   Toss all the ingredients together. Let the garlic flavor the tomatoes for a few minutes.

6   Taste for salt and add more to your preferred taste.

7   Remove the garlic.

8   Spread the tomato mixture on the toasted bread and serve immediately.

THE GAS STATION VEGAN

When I was in my early twenties, I was in a relationship with a man named Rick who was in a very popular punk band that used to tour all around the United States. I would often travel with him, meaning that we drove across the United States several times. This was in the very early 2000s, when, I quickly learned, it was difficult, if not nearly impossible, to be vegan in Middle America. So I came up with a plan: How to Make Vegan Food on the Road, and I even wanted to write a book called *The Gas Station Vegan* (because we were always stopping for gas). There I would grab juice, nuts, and some condiments, like tiny packets of hot sauce, and whip out my tiny portable propane grill and somehow manage to make an entire meal.

I came up with the idea for this grilled tofu: I'd marinate the tofu in lemon juice, olive oil, and herbs and then grill it, topping the tofu with arugula and some smashed-up gas station salted nuts and many packets of hot sauce! Rick (who was not vegan by any means but loved to eat everything I made even when it was random things thrown together) and I learned that you can make delicious dishes without having access to fancy ingredients and fancy equipment. Sometimes all you need is a little tiny portable grill.

Organic tofu is one of the cleanest and most basic forms of plant-based protein. However, it doesn't really taste like anything in particular on its own, so you have to treat it with some love, skill, and patience. But if you give yourself the time, and if you marinate it with the right spices and herbs, you can create some truly incredible, totally craveable protein additions to your meal.

GRILLED CITRUS HERB TOFU

SERVES 4 TO 6

My favorite way to cook tofu is to grill it over an open flame to produce those nice black markings and that slightly charred taste that most people love.

If you don't want to use an open flame, you can use a cast-iron griddle pan.

1 cup extra-virgin olive oil

½ cup lemon juice

½ cup tamari

¼ cup minced garlic

2 tablespoons chopped fresh basil

2 tablespoons chopped fresh dill

2 tablespoons chopped fresh parsley

1½ teaspoons black pepper

1 pound block super firm tofu (I love Wildwood and Hodo brands)

1   In a high-speed blender, combine the olive oil, lemon juice, tamari, garlic, basil, dill, parsley, and pepper. Blend for 1 minute, or until smooth.

2   Cut the tofu into ¼- to ½-inch thick rectangles, slicing from the narrow end of the block. Pat the excess water from the tofu with a clean kitchen cloth or a paper towel to allow for better absorption of the olive oil mixture.

3   Arrange the tofu in a bowl. Pour the olive oil mixture over the tofu and turn it to coat. Marinate the tofu in the refrigerator for a minimum of 4 hours, turning the tofu about halfway through.

4   Grill the marinated tofu on each side until beautiful black grill marks appear.

TIP: This tofu is best served with Roasted Garlic Aioli (page 48) and fresh Gremolata (page 45).

GIGANTE BEANS

SERVES 6 TO 8

You will always want to include a bean salad when serving antipasti. I chose gigante beans here, which are actually a Greek variety of large lima beans. I love their fleshy, meaty texture. However, if you cannot find gigante beans, butter beans or cannellini beans are the best alternative.

In a large bowl, mix together the beans, olive oil, basil, lemon juice, garlic, coriander, salt, pepper, and chili flakes. Be careful not to break the beans. Serve on an antipasti plate alongside a few of the other recipes in this section.

3 cups gigante beans, cooked or canned

6 tablespoons extra-virgin olive oil

2 tablespoons chopped fresh basil

1 tablespoon lemon juice

1½ teaspoons chopped garlic

1½ teaspoons ground coriander

¼ teaspoon sea salt

¼ teaspoon black pepper

Pinch of chili flakes

POLPETTINE

(MEATBALLS)

SERVES 6 TO 8

Both sides of my family generally cooked meatballs on a weekly basis. We constantly argued about whose tasted better, but we all secretly knew that my dad's mother had the best recipe.

My grandmother eventually passed her recipe on to my mom. Thereafter, every Sunday morning the whole house smelled like garlic and oil and simmering tomatoes, all so fragrant and mouthwatering. I wish I could turn that smell into a candle.

When I became vegan, I could no longer eat those wonderful meatballs, so I needed to figure out a way to veganize them. After many failures, I finally came up with a winning combination of lentils and mushrooms. Mushrooms are too watery to stand on their own, so the lentils are necessary to add texture and stiffness—but if you prefer other beans instead of lentils, feel free to use them.

In the recipe below I recommend cremini mushrooms, but you can also try portobello or any other type you enjoy. The final result will feature the garlic, the grated "cheese" (we use nutritional yeast), parsley, and all the flavor profiles my grandmother used, but without meat.

1 cup dry lentils

2 tablespoons extra-virgin olive oil, plus ¼ cup

1 pound cremini mushrooms, sliced

2 tablespoons minced garlic

½ cup finely diced yellow onion

3¼ teaspoons sea salt

⅓ cup sunflower seeds

1 cup vital wheat gluten

2 tablespoons nutritional yeast

1 teaspoon smoked paprika

1 teaspoon dried oregano

1 teaspoon black pepper

3 cups panko

1 cup chopped fresh parsley

---

1 Rinse the dry lentils in a strainer. Pick through and remove any debris or rocks. Rinse thoroughly under running water. Transfer the lentils to a small saucepan and add 3 cups of water. Bring to a rapid boil over medium-high heat. Once boiling, reduce the heat to maintain a gentle simmer. Simmer uncovered for 20 to 30 minutes or until tender. Stir in ¼ teaspoon of the salt. Set aside and let cool as you prepare the meatballs.

Continued

2   Heat 2 tablespoons of olive oil in a small sauté pan. Sauté the mushrooms, 1 tablespoon of the garlic, the onion, and 1 teaspoon of the salt over medium heat for 10 to 12 minutes.

3   Preheat the oven to 350°F. Generously oil a baking sheet.

4   Place the cooked lentils, sunflower seeds, 1 tablespoon of garlic, ¼ cup of the olive oil, wheat gluten, yeast, paprika, oregano, pepper, and the remaining 2 teaspoons of salt in a food processor and blend until you get a sticky, dough-like consistency.

5   Add 2 cups of the cooked cremini mushroom mixture to the food processor and blend together until smooth.

6   In a large mixing bowl, combine the blended ingredients with the remaining cooked mushrooms, then add the panko and parsley.

7   Using a 1½-ounce scoop (or 2 heaping tablespoons), or with your hands, roll the mixture into tight little balls. Place them on the baking sheet.

8   Bake the meatballs for 20 minutes, flipping them over after 10 minutes.

9   Drown in marinara sauce and serve alongside Baked Ricotta (page 60) or your favorite pasta.

TIP: Don't skimp on garlic, and make sure you have a huge batch of sauce to dunk the meatballs into. They are best when completely soaking in sauce.

ARANCINI

SERVES 6 TO 8 ✦ **MAKES APPROXIMATELY 4 DOZEN ARANCINI**

Arancini are breaded and fried rice balls, a typical Sicilian street food. They weren't part of my family's daily menu, but I fell in love with them when I lived in Rome, where they are called *suppli*. Normally arancini are served as a snack or an appetizer, and in Sicily you can find people selling them out of carts everywhere.

You can make the risotto part of this recipe and eat it as risotto, but if you want more, why not try these amazing little treats? Stick the arancini in the fridge and reheat them in the oven at 350°F until the center is hot, about 15 minutes.

RISOTTO

¼ cup, plus 2 teaspoons extra-virgin olive oil

2 tablespoons vegan salted butter

2 cups finely diced yellow onion

1 cup finely diced shallots

1 cup finely diced celery

2 tablespoons minced garlic

1 tablespoon smoked paprika

2 teaspoons sea salt, plus 1 teaspoon to taste

2 cups carnaroli or Arborio rice

1 cup dry white wine

4 cups vegetable stock

⅓ cup lemon juice

½ cup Cashew Mozzarella (page 34)

4 cups Cashew Cream (page 56)

2½ tablespoons egg replacer

4 cups panko (or Pangrattato, page 51)

Avocado, grapeseed, or rice bran oil for frying

1 Make the risotto: In a sauté pan, heat the olive oil and vegan butter over medium heat. Sauté the onion, shallots, celery, garlic, smoked paprika, and salt for 5 to 7 minutes, until the onion is translucent.

2 Add the rice and sauté for 2 to 3 minutes.

3 Add the wine and cook for 3 to 4 minutes, stirring constantly.

4 Slowly add the stock, 1 cup at a time, stirring constantly. Bring the rice to a low boil.

5 When the rice is fully cooked, remove it from the heat. Stir in the lemon juice and remaining 2 teaspoons of olive oil and mix well. Add salt to taste.

You can stop here if you just want to make risotto, a Northern Italian specialty—there are two more risotto recipes, Risotto Pomodoro on page 206 and Heartbeet Risotto on page 207.

6 After the risotto has cooled, use a 2-ounce ice cream or dough scoop and divide the rice into little balls. If you don't have a scoop, roll ¼ cup of rice into balls with your hands.

Continued

7   Take ½ teaspoon of cashew mozzarella and insert it into the center of each rice ball. Using your hands, close up the rice balls neatly.

8   To make the batter, place the cashew cream in a bowl and add the egg replacer. Whip until thick.

9   Place the panko in a separate bowl. Dip each rice ball into the batter, letting the excess batter drip off.

10 Roll each ball in the panko, making sure to coat it all the way around. Set aside.

11 Add about an inch of the frying oil to a large frying pan.

12 Heat the oil to 360° to 375°F. Use a deep-fry thermometer to make sure the oil is hot enough.

13 Fry a few rice balls at a time. Do not crowd the pan. Make sure the balls do not touch, so they don't stick together. Fry for approximately 3 minutes, or until golden brown and crispy.

14 Remove the balls from the oil and place them on paper towels to drain.

TIP: Serve with Marinara Sauce (page 37) for dipping.

GARLIC PARMIGIANO POTATO WEDGES

SERVES 4 TO 6

Most cultures, including Italian, serve some variety of potatoes. My parents and grandparents made potatoes in dozens of different ways, but I believe that the simplest way is also sometimes the best (and the most craveable). So, for these potato wedges, I basically copied what my mother used. She also liked to add a little bit of parmigiano cheese, but she stopped doing that once I became vegan.

Now, however, we have our Macadamia Parmigiano (page 35), so you can put that on top along with the Roasted Garlic Aioli (page 48).

3 pounds Yukon gold potatoes

½ cup extra-virgin olive oil

1 tablespoon minced garlic

1 tablespoon sea salt

2 teaspoons finely chopped fresh rosemary leaves

1 teaspoon black pepper

1 teaspoon onion powder

1 teaspoon smoked paprika

1 teaspoon paprika

Macadamia Parmigiano (page 35), for topping

1   Preheat the oven to 350°F.

2   Cut the potatoes into ¾-inch-thick wedges.

3   In a large bowl, mix together the olive oil, garlic, salt, rosemary, pepper, onion powder, and paprikas.

4   Add the potatoes. Toss, making sure to coat each piece well.

5   Place the potatoes on a baking sheet. Bake for 25 to 30 minutes. Test the potatoes for doneness by sticking a fork through the thickest piece. If the fork goes straight through, the potato is tender, and you are ready to serve.

6   Sprinkle the potatoes with macadamia parmigiano and watch them disappear!

TIP: These potato wedges can be served with a number of different sauces. Try them with my favorite, Roasted Garlic Aioli (page 48).

CROCCHETTE DI PATATE

SERVES 6 TO 8

I challenge you to find somebody who doesn't like potatoes! I adore them, especially because you can cook them in so many different ways: boil them, bake them, mash them, fry them—do whatever you want with them and they're always great.

These potatoes are a take on a Calabrian version of the crocchette. I zhuzh them up a little bit to make them more interesting by adding a small amount of Cashew Mozzarella (page 34).

These are perfect fried, but they're also excellent baked.

4 pounds potatoes (Yukon gold preferred, russet next best)

1 tablespoon sea salt, plus more as needed

1 tablespoon black pepper

1 tablespoon minced garlic

½ cup finely chopped fresh parsley

1½ cups Cashew Mozzarella (page 34), cut into ¼-inch cubes

1 cup all-purpose flour

4 cups Cashew Cream (page 56)

2½ tablespoons egg replacer

4 cups panko

Avocado, grapeseed, or rice bran oil for frying

1   Prepare the potatoes: Preheat the oven to 450°F. Poke each potato all over with a fork. Wrap the potatoes in aluminum foil. Bake until soft, 45 to 55 minutes, depending on the size of the potatoes.

2   Let the potatoes cool. Remove the skins. Put the potatoes through a food mill or mash extremely well with a potato masher.

3   In a large mixing bowl, combine the potatoes, salt, pepper, garlic, and parsley. Mix well by hand or with a sturdy mixing spoon. Taste for salt.

4   Gently fold in the cashew mozzarella cubes.

5   Using a 2-ounce scoop, portion the potato mixture into balls, then shape them into ovals.

6   Pour the flour into a separate bowl.

7   Roll each crocchette in the flour.

8   To make the batter, pour the cashew cream into a large bowl. Stir in the egg replacer and whip until thick.

9   Pour the panko into another bowl.

TIP: If you do not have panko, use your Pangrattato (page 51) for the breading!

10 Dip each crocchette individually into the batter, letting the excess drip off. Then roll them in the panko, making sure to completely coat them. Set aside.

11 Add about an inch of the oil to a large frying pan. Heat the oil to 360° to 375°F. Use a deep-fry thermometer to make sure the oil is hot enough.

12 Fry a few crocchette at a time. Do not crowd the pan. Make sure they do not touch, so they don't stick together. Fry for approximately 3 minutes, or until golden brown and crispy.

13 Remove from the oil and place on a paper towel to drain.

CALABRIAN STUFFED CHERRY PEPPERS

SERVES 4 TO 6

A traditional Calabrian treat, these are best if you enjoy a little heat, but of course they can be made with sweet peppers to avoid spice. Cherry peppers in jars are found in most supermarkets and are available in mild or hot varieties.

12 cherry peppers

1 cup Tuna Salad (page 84)

¼ cup capers in vinegar

1 tablespoon chopped fresh parsley

Extra-virgin olive oil for drizzling

1 Drain the cherry peppers.

2 Cut the stems out of the peppers. Remove the seeds with a very small spoon or knife, being careful not to cut into the peppers. Turn the peppers upside down on a kitchen towel and let them dry out for a few minutes.

3 Fill a plastic disposable piping bag with the tuna salad. You can use a small spoon if you do not have a piping bag.

4 Fill each pepper to the top with the tuna.

5 Top the stuffed peppers with a few capers (as many as your taste desires), the parsley, and a drizzle of olive oil. Add these to your beautifully colorful antipasti platter.

CROSTINI

SERVES 4 TO 6

Crostini are small toasts spread with various toppings and might just be the easiest and most fun snack, appetizer, or treat for parties. Crostini can be made in so many different ways, so you can tailor each type to your or your guests' desires. You can do savory. You can do sweet. You can do sweet and savory together.

My own favorite is tuna crostini using Tuna Salad (page 84) with fresh tomatoes or capers. I also like putting a bit of Almond Ricotta (page 33) with fresh slices of strawberries and a drizzle of balsamic glaze. Find the best quality Italian bread at your local bakery. Sourdough would work as well.

Small loaf of Italian bread

½ cup extra-virgin olive oil

2 teaspoons minced garlic

Pinch of sea salt

Tiny pinch of black pepper

Pinch of chili flakes (optional)

1   Cut the bread into ¼- to ½-inch slices.

2   In a medium bowl, mix the olive oil, garlic, salt, pepper, and chili flakes, if using.

3   Dip a pastry brush in the oil mixture. Brush one side of each slice of bread lightly with the oil (or heavily, depending on your desired taste).

4   Place the slices in a toaster oven, set on toast, or broil in a regular stove until golden brown. If you use the stove, do not walk too far away. It only takes a minute or two before you could burn your toast!

TIP: Once you have your perfect little toasts, you are ready! Be creative— you can make so many different versions of crostini. Strawberry Almond Ricotta (page 80) and Sicilian Tuna (page 83) are my favorites.

STRAWBERRY ALMOND RICOTTA CROSTINI

MAKES 1 SLICE

The perfect amount of sweetness. The perfect amount of savory. The perfect amount of zing. The perfect amount of crunch. These crostini will win over your toughest critics! They are an absolute must to serve at any gathering.

1 slice of crostino (see page 79)

1 tablespoon Almond Ricotta (page 33)

3 to 5 slices fresh strawberries

Pinch of Maldon salt

Balsamic glaze

Microbasil or torn fresh basil

1   Spread the almond ricotta on the crostino.

2   Slice the strawberries and evenly place them on the ricotta.

3   Sprinkle the Maldon salt on the strawberries (a tiny pinch of plain sea salt is okay, but the Maldon salt adds a perfect crunch).

4   Drizzle balsamic glaze on top—a little goes a very long way—and top with basil.

SICILIAN TUNA CROSTINI

MAKES 1 SLICE

Sophisticated, refined, and delightfully rich and crispy, these crostini will excite your guests once you tell them you made the tuna yourself using nuts and other simple ingredients! This is the perfect appetizer for any gathering, as it seconds as a conversation piece. Get them talking!

1 slice of crostino (page 79)

1 tablespoon Tuna Salad (page 84)

3 to 5 grape or cherry tomato halves

Tiny pinch of Maldon salt

Chopped fresh parsley

Capers or sliced caper berries

1   Spread the tuna salad on top of the crostino.

2   Place the tomato halves across the top.

3   Sprinkle the Maldon salt on the tomatoes.

4   Sprinkle with parsley and finish with a few capers on top. Or if you prefer (and if you can find them), top with a sliced caper berry for a lighter taste.

TUNA SALAD

SERVES 6 TO 8

When I was young, my mother never allowed me to eat food from the school cafeteria; instead, every morning she made me lunch. My classmates were super jealous. I would always have a sandwich, a thermos full of homemade soup, and, of course, a chocolate chip cookie because what kid can go through a day of school without a chocolate chip cookie?

Tuna salad was my sandwich of choice because, even as a child, I was grossed out by cold cuts. They seemed weird and slimy and gross. Luckily, my mother made bomb tuna, the best ever. I don't know what she did to it, because it came out of the same can everyone else bought. That tuna salad sandwich was one of the foods I most craved as a vegan: something about the celery and the onion, the crunch and the texture.

I eventually designed my equivalent version of tuna, which technically is an all raw, oil-free recipe for the actual tuna itself. But my preferred version of the sandwich is grilling the tuna a little and making a tuna melt for a wonderful flashback into my childhood.

¾ cup raw, unsalted cashews

4 cups raw, unsalted almonds

2 cups finely diced onion

2 cups finely diced celery

1 cup packed fresh parsley leaves, minced

¼ cup lemon juice, plus 6 tablespoons

Pinch of cayenne

5 ounces avocado (by weight; approximately 1 avocado)

1 teaspoon dulse flakes

1½ teaspoons sea salt, plus more if needed

1 teaspoon minced garlic

3 tablespoons apple cider vinegar

1½ teaspoons chopped nori

---

1   Soak the cashews in water for a minimum of 4 hours. Drain and rinse well. Set aside.

2   Make the tuna: In a food processor, pulse the almonds until they are a fine crumble (not paste). Add the almond mixture to a large bowl. Stir in the onion, celery, parsley, ¼ cup of lemon juice, and cayenne. Set aside.

3   Make the mayo: Add the prepared cashews, avocado, the remaining 6 tablespoons of lemon juice, dulse, salt, garlic, vinegar, and nori to the container of a high-speed blender. Blend until smooth. Add a tiny bit of filtered water if necessary.

4   Add the mayo to the bowl with the tuna and mix well. Add salt to taste if needed.

STUFFED MUSHROOMS OREGANATA

SERVES 4 TO 6

These stuffed mushrooms were on the table for every single holiday when I was growing up. They are savory, crunchy, and extremely satisfying. Best of all, they're really easy to make!

12 to 15 cremini mushrooms, depending on size

2 cups Pangrattato (page 51)

½ cup nutritional yeast

1 tablespoon minced garlic

½ cup chopped fresh parsley

1½ teaspoons chopped fresh mint

1½ teaspoons dried oregano

1½ teaspoons sea salt

1½ teaspoons black pepper

¼ cup lemon juice

½ cup extra-virgin olive oil, plus more for drizzling

½ cup vegan butter, melted

1   Preheat the oven to 350°F. Oil a baking sheet.

2   Wipe the mushrooms with a damp cloth and remove the stems to create a cavity.

3   Make the stuffing: In a large bowl, mix together the pangrattato, yeast, garlic, parsley, mint, oregano, salt, pepper, lemon juice, olive oil, and vegan butter.

4   Turn the mushroom caps upside down. Spoon the stuffing into each mushroom to fill the cavity.

5   Arrange the mushrooms, stuffing side up, on the prepared baking sheet. Drizzle with olive oil.

6   Bake for 15 minutes, or until fully cooked and crispy on top.

ROASTED GARLIC CANNELLINI BEAN DIP

MAKES 6 CUPS

Whenever you have a party, offering a selection of excellent dips can make a delicious difference—but dips can also be wonderful simply when you don't feel like eating a full dinner or when you just want a snack. There are thousands of possibilities here, but one of my very favorites is cannellini dip.

You can replace cannellini beans with fava beans, chickpeas, or borlotti beans (or any other bean that suits your taste). You just have to pay attention to seasoning them correctly and making them the right texture.

4 cups Cannellini Beans (page 49)

½ cup Roasted Garlic (page 46)

2 tablespoons tahini

½ cup lemon juice

1 cup extra-virgin olive oil, plus more for drizzling

½ teaspoon black pepper

1 teaspoon sea salt, plus more to taste

4 to 6 leaves fresh basil, chopped, plus extra for garnish

1 to 2 teaspoons chopped fresh parsley, plus extra for garnish

1 teaspoon fresh rosemary leaves, plus more for garnish

TIP: Canned cannellini beans are okay to use for this recipe, but cooking dry cannellini beans always tastes and feels better once you have done the prep.

1 Place the beans, garlic, tahini, lemon juice, olive oil, pepper, and salt in a food processor and blend on high until completely smooth. Transfer to a bowl.

2 Fold the basil, parsley, and rosemary into the cannellini bean mixture. Season with salt as needed. To make it look special, garnish with a sprinkle of basil, parsley, and rosemary to take the dip to the next level.

3 When you're ready to serve, top with a drizzle of olive oil.

4 Serve with Grilled Ciabatta Garlic Bread (page 54).

INSALATA E VERDURE

Sautéed Swiss Chard with Cannellini Beans, *Page 105*

CAPRESE

SERVES 4 TO 6

There are few dishes more appetizing than a caprese salad using sweet, ripe, juicy tomatoes and nice fresh mozzarella. As a vegan, I would watch others eat this salad and be jealous because I wanted it so badly. So I knew it was imperative to create a vegan mozzarella in a way that would be complementary to the luscious tomatoes. I think I nailed it. My customers at the restaurant seem to agree!

3 cups Cashew Mozzarella (page 34)

2 heirloom tomatoes (any variety will do, but I prefer the red and purple ones)

12 to 15 large leaves fresh basil

Extra-virgin olive oil

Balsamic glaze

Maldon salt for topping

Freshly ground black pepper for topping

---

1   Pour the cashew mozzarella into a small rectangular baking pan.

2   Cover the mozzarella with a sheet of parchment paper. Place any pan or dish that fits exactly inside the baking pan on top of the parchment paper. Refrigerate the cheese for 4 hours. Weighting the cheese will provide the best texture for your caprese mozzarella.

3   Remove the weight and the parchment paper. Cut circles from the mozzarella with a 3-inch-diameter drinking glass (or a 3-inch-wide round mold).

4   Drizzle the mozzarella with a little olive oil to prevent sticking.

5   Place your hand over the top end of the cheese and hold it steady. Using a sharp knife, cut approximately ¼- to ½-inch-thick slices from right to left evenly. Continue cutting into perfect little circles until you reach your desired number of mozzarella circles.

6   Save the ends/scraps for another dish. We don't waste food around here!

7   Cut the tomatoes crosswise into slightly thicker slices than the mozzarella.

8   Arrange the tomatoes and mozzarella on a serving platter, alternating the slices of tomatoes and cheese. Tuck a basil leaf between the slices.

9   Drizzle with ample olive oil and a swizzle of balsamic glaze, then sprinkle with Maldon salt and a few twists of pepper.

TRICOLORE

SERVES 6 TO 8

When I was growing up, our family always ate a salad after we ate our pasta—that's the order of how dishes are served in Italy. But when I started working at Pure Food and Wine, I learned that it was healthier for your digestion to eat salad before the main course—the roughage clears the path for the heavier foods to come.

A tricolore salad is a blend of arugula, radicchio, and Belgian endive—exactly as my mother always made it, using whatever other lettuces were in season—along with a really good balsamic dressing. That's the key to this salad: a vinaigrette made of the best balsamic vinegar and olive oils you can afford. If you use an excellent quality, cold-pressed extra-virgin olive oil, which has peppery notes, along with a nicely aged balsamic vinegar, you will take your salad to the next level.

---

3 cups Belgian endive

3 cups radicchio

6 cups arugula

Balsamic Vinaigrette (recipe follows)

Macadamia Parmigiano (page 35)

Garlic Croutons (page 55, optional)

BALSAMIC VINAIGRETTE

Makes approximately 2 cups

¾ cup balsamic vinegar

1 tablespoon Dijon or stone-ground mustard (not yellow!)

1½ teaspoons agave syrup

1½ teaspoons minced garlic

½ teaspoon sea salt

½ teaspoon black pepper

¾ cup extra-virgin olive oil

SALAD

1   Cut the stems off the endive. (If prepping ahead of time, squirt lemon juice on the endive to prevent it from turning brown.) Cut it into ¼-inch pieces. Cut the stems off the radicchio and chop it into ¼-inch pieces.

2   Place the endive and radicchio in a salad bowl and add the arugula. Add balsamic vinaigrette to taste and toss the salad.

3   Top with macadamia parmigiano to taste and garlic croutons, if using.

BALSAMIC VINAIGRETTE

1   In a high-speed blender, combine the vinegar, mustard, agave syrup, garlic, salt, and pepper. Blend for 45 to 60 seconds.

2   With the blender running, slowly add the olive oil so the mixture emulsifies. You will know it is emulsifying when you see the color and texture change to appear creamy.

3   You can store leftover vinaigrette in the refrigerator for up to a week.

CESARE

Caesar salad is the pride of Tijuana, Mexico, but was of course created there by an Italian named Caesar Cardini. When it's good, it's heaven. I happen to think that at Pura Vita we have the absolute best Caesar salad in the world. That's it, I'm sticking to it.

There are several ways you can mix up this salad. You can make it gluten free, you can make it with ciabatta croutons, or you could use yam croutons (I include the recipe here). What's really important is the dressing and the massaging of the kale. Remember: You've got to massage your kale. Your kale is very stressed out. It needs to relax.

SALAD

1   Wash and dry the kale. Remove the thick part of the stem by cutting down the sides of the stem and removing it.

2   Stack the kale leaves on top of each other, roll them up, and cut them into thin strips.

NOTE: If you would like to use Romaine instead of, or with, kale, prep your romaine lettuce as follows: Cut the core end of the romaine off and discard. Slice the head of romaine in half lengthwise to create two long halves of lettuce. Turn the cut side down and slice the lettuce again lengthwise into quarters. Chop the lettuce into 1-inch pieces starting from the leafy end. Wash well after cutting by putting the lettuce pieces in a colander and rinse thoroughly under cold water. Blot with a paper towel or use a salad spinner to dry the lettuce before using.

3   In a mixing bowl, combine the kale and Cesare dressing and mix. Using food-handling gloves, massage the kale with your hands to break down the raw kale and make it more palatable.

4   Once the kale has a nice, relaxing massage, put it in the salad bowl. Add the chickpeas and croutons. Sprinkle with macadamia parmigiano and dulse to taste.

5   Serve with a lemon slice for a little extra zing.

Continued

4 cups kale or romaine lettuce, or a mix of half and half

2 to 3 tablespoons Cesare Dressing (recipe follows)

¼ cup precooked or canned chickpeas

¼ cup Garlic Croutons (page 55) or Yam Croutons (recipe follows)

Macadamia Parmigiano (page 35) for serving

Dulse flakes for serving

Lemon slices for serving (optional)

CESARE DRESSING

Makes approximately 1½ cups

¼ cup raw, unsalted cashews

¼ cup raw, unsalted almonds

3 tablespoons lemon juice

2 tablespoons tamari

¼ cup filtered water

1 tablespoon stone-ground or Dijon mustard

1 tablespoon nutritional yeast

1 tablespoon finely chopped shallot

½ teaspoon minced garlic

¼ teaspoon black pepper

Pinch of dulse flakes

2 tablespoons extra-virgin olive oil

CESARE DRESSING

1   Soak the cashews and almonds in water for a minimum of 4 hours. Drain and rinse well before using.

2   Combine the cashews, almonds, lemon juice, tamari, water, mustard, yeast, shallot, garlic, pepper, and dulse in a high-powered blender and blend on medium-high speed until smooth.

3   With the blender running on low, slowly add the olive oil to emulsify the dressing.

4   Add a little more filtered water if the dressing becomes too thick.

TIP: You can refrigerate or freeze the Cesare dressing for later use. It is excellent on raw vegetables—use it as a dip for crudités.

YAM CROUTONS

1   Preheat the oven to 350°F.

2   Wash and peel the yam. Cut it into ½-inch cubes.

3   In a mixing bowl, toss the yams with the olive oil, garlic, salt, and pepper.

4   Spread them on a medium baking sheet.

5   Roast for 30 to 35 minutes, flipping them occasionally. Be sure they are cooked all the way through but not too crispy.

YAM CROUTONS

Makes 2 cups

1 large yam

1 tablespoon extra-virgin olive oil

1 teaspoon minced garlic

½ teaspoon sea salt

½ teaspoon black pepper

VERDE

SERVES 1 TO 2

This verde salad is so simple you can make it anytime. All you need are the greens and some fresh herbs. It's the perfect way to start or end your meal, depending on which order you prefer to eat your dishes.

SALAD

Place the lettuce, arugula, tarragon, and mint in a serving bowl. Add the dressing and toss. Top with the avocado, spiced pepitas, and garlic croutons, if using.

AGED SHERRY VINAIGRETTE

Mix the vinegar, mustard, shallots, agave syrup, salt, and pepper in a high-speed blender. With the blender running on low, slowly pour in the olive oil to emulsify the dressing. The vinaigrette can be refrigerated for approximately 5 to 6 days.

2 cups washed and torn butter lettuce

1 cup arugula

1 tablespoon chopped fresh tarragon

1 tablespoon chopped fresh mint

1 tablespoon Aged Sherry Vinaigrette (recipe follows)

½ avocado, diced, for topping

2 teaspoons Spiced Pepitas (page 57) for topping

Garlic Croutons for topping (page 55, optional)

AGED SHERRY VINAIGRETTE

Makes approximately 1½ cups

½ cup aged sherry vinegar

1 tablespoon Dijon mustard

1½ tablespoons chopped shallots

½ tablespoon agave syrup

¼ teaspoon sea salt

¼ teaspoon black pepper

¾ cup extra-virgin olive oil

PANZANELLA

There are many summer salads, but panzanella is simply one of the best. My mom made it every year as soon as the tomatoes were available, tossing them with whatever leftover bread she had from the night before. With a nice vinaigrette, it's simple: just thinly sliced onions and fresh, beautiful summer tomatoes oozing their sweet juices, all of it soaked up by the slightly crunchy stale bread.

1 large heirloom tomato, cut into bite-sized pieces, or 12 cherry tomatoes, halved

1 cup Garlic Croutons (page 55)

2 tablespoons torn basil

1 tablespoon very thinly sliced red onion, or to taste

3 tablespoons Red Wine Vinaigrette (recipe follows)

Pinch of Maldon salt

Microbasil for garnish (optional)

SALAD

1 Cut the tomato into ½-inch to ¾-inch pieces or quarters, whichever you prefer. You should have about 1 cup.

2 Place the tomatoes, croutons, basil, and red onion in a serving bowl. Add the dressing and toss.

3 Let the salad sit in the dressing for at least 20 minutes before serving. You want the croutons to soak up some dressing before you eat!

4 Top with a little pinch of Maldon salt and garnish with microbasil, if using.

RED WINE VINAIGRETTE

1 Add the vinegar, mustard, agave syrup, garlic, salt, and pepper to a high-speed blender. Mix until blended. With the blender running on low, slowly pour in the olive oil to emulsify the dressing. The vinaigrette can be refrigerated for approximately 5 to 6 days.

RED WINE VINAIGRETTE

Makes approximately 1½ cups

½ cup red wine vinegar

½ tablespoon Dijon mustard

½ tablespoon agave syrup

½ tablespoon minced garlic

½ teaspoon sea salt

½ teaspoon black pepper

1 cup extra-virgin olive oil

HEIRLOOM TOMATO *and* WATERMELON SALAD

SERVES 1 TO 2

I love watermelon. I can't even count the number of ways I can add watermelon to make any dish better. You can also eat it as is, or quick grilled with spices, such as chili powder or smoked salt. Just about anything!

This watermelon and tomato salad is particularly refreshing because the watermelon and tomato complement each other well and the almond ricotta adds texture. It's a fresh and very summery dish to serve to guests (or just for yourself, for a special treat). Just remember to keep it chilled.

2 cups watermelon (chopped into 1-inch pieces)

1 cup diced heirloom tomato, or halved cherry or grape tomatoes

¼ cup torn fresh basil

2 tablespoons Aged Sherry Vinaigrette (page 97)

1½ teaspoons chopped fresh tarragon

1 tablespoon Almond Ricotta (page 33)

1 tablespoon Roasted Pistachio Crumble (page 42)

Balsamic glaze for drizzling

Pinch of Maldon salt

---

1 Place the watermelon, tomatoes, and basil in a serving bowl. Stir the tarragon into the sherry vinaigrette and toss.

2 Top with the almond ricotta, pistachio crumble, balsamic glaze, and salt.

BROCCOLI RABE

SERVES 4 TO 6

While popular in Europe, broccoli rabe is not familiar to most Americans. It's a bitter Italian broccoli, and the one place in America where broccoli rabe is popular is the New York City area, with its large Italian American population. While I was growing up, our family often ate broccoli rabe during the week alongside pasta, but we always had it on Sundays, and often with the Peppas (page 106).

When I moved to Los Angeles, I was surprised to find how very few people ate broccoli rabe; when I opened the restaurant and put it on the menu, no one ordered it—ever. But I couldn't in good faith have an Italian restaurant that didn't serve broccoli rabe, so we started giving it out to diners to taste as a sidenote to whatever else they were ordering. Three months later, we couldn't make it fast enough; people loved it—and still do.

One of the best parts of broccoli rabe is that it's so easy to make. You don't have to do much to it except blanch it, which removes some of the bitterness and helps clean the vegetable.

Make sure to cut off the big, thick stems. Then you can keep the broccoli rabe whole or cut it into smaller pieces. You can't go wrong, not with my favorite vegetable in the whole world.

3 bunches broccoli rabe

1 tablespoon garlic, minced or sliced paper-thin

½ cup extra-virgin olive oil

2 teaspoons sea salt

Pinch of chili flakes

---

1   To blanch the broccoli rabe, bring a large pot of water to a boil. Place the broccoli rabe into the boiling water and cook for 2 minutes.

2   Immediately remove from the water and toss into an ice bath. Drain.

3   Cut off approximately 2 inches of the bottom of the stems.

4   In a sauté pan, sauté the garlic in the olive oil over a low flame for 2 to 3 minutes. Do not burn the garlic!

5   Add the broccoli rabe, salt, and chili flakes. Sauté for 6 to 8 minutes, until the broccoli rabe is tender but not soft. Add more salt if necessary.

SAUTÉED SPINACH

SERVES 1 TO 2

Simple and fast to make, sautéed spinach complements nearly every dish. Everyone needs to eat more greens. This easy recipe gives you zero excuses.

2 tablespoons extra-virgin olive oil

1 garlic clove, sliced as thin as possible

Pinch of sea salt

Pinch of black pepper

2 teaspoons aged balsamic vinegar

4 cups raw baby spinach

1   In a large sauté pan over medium-low heat, sauté the olive oil with the garlic, salt, pepper, and vinegar for 2 to 3 minutes.

2   Add the spinach and cook for approximately 5 minutes. It will wilt down to a small amount, so feel free to double this recipe!

SAUTÉED SWISS CHARD
with CANNELLINI BEANS

SERVES 4 TO 6

This sautéed vegetable and bean dish is a traditional offering in Calabria, the most southern region of Italy, where my grandmother is from. I like to use Swiss chard, which is the easiest to find and cook, although you can use other types of greens, such as turnip leaves or escarole if you like this dish a bit more bitter.

The greens need to be thoroughly chopped or ripped apart, whichever you prefer.

For the beans, I prefer cannellini or butter beans, as fat white ones are the best for this dish. You can, of course, use beans from a can, making sure to drain all the liquid, or you can cook your beans. If that's the case, make sure you use fresh dried beans. Check the expiration date. Old beans take forever to cook and they never taste as good.

¼ cup extra-virgin olive oil, plus more for drizzling

2 whole garlic cloves, smashed

4 to 5 cups Swiss chard, cut into 2- to 3-inch pieces

2 tablespoons lemon juice

½ teaspoon sea salt

½ teaspoon black pepper

2 Calabrian chilis

1 cup precooked cannellini beans

Maldon salt

TIP: This dish is best made with fresh beans, so plan ahead and follow the recipe for Cannellini Beans (page 49).

TIP: Be sure to prep your Swiss chard by washing it well. Chard can sometimes hold dirt in its crevices, so give it a good rinse.

1   In a sauté pan, sauté the garlic in the olive oil over low to medium heat for 3 to 4 minutes. Be careful not to burn the garlic.

2   Add the chard to the pan. Sauté until the chard is fully cooked, 4 to 5 minutes. The chard will wilt down considerably.

3   Add the lemon juice, salt, pepper, and chilis. Feel free to use fewer chilis or eliminate them completely.

4   Add the precooked beans and sauté them. Toss everything around until all is mixed well and piping hot. Transfer to a serving bowl.

5   Drizzle with olive oil.

6   As always, I love my Maldon salt, so sprinkle away to your desired taste and dig in.

PEPPAS

SERVES 6 TO 8

My dad is obsessed with hot peppers, but the ones he loves the most are the Italian long hots. In each batch, most of the peppers are spicy, but there are always one or two that are so ridiculously hot they could almost melt your tongue. We used to wait and see which of us got that one, because only my dad and I could tolerate that tremendous amount of heat. It was our special bond. If my brother ate the hot one, he would swear off peppers for at least three months. My mother was smart: She didn't eat them at all.

Now that both my dad and I live on the West Coast, where these Italian long hots aren't sold, friends back East will send us cases of them. You can't freeze the peppers, so when they arrive, we try to eat them all right away.

The peppers in this recipe are not as hot as the ones my dad loves. Here we use mini sweet peppers mixed with California Fresno chilis, which are spicier. But you can use any peppers you want for this dish, although I would avoid green bells, as they are too bitter. I recommend making a big batch, as it will last throughout the week. Try the peppers on pasta, put some in a sandwich, or just eat as is.

---

1. Preheat the oven to 350°F.

2. Cut the sweet peppers into approximately 1-inch round pieces. Or, if you prefer, you can leave the sweet peppers whole, to present them in their full beauty.

3. Slice the Fresno chilis into approximately ¼-inch round, thin pieces. Remove the seeds.

4. In a large bowl, toss the peppers with the garlic, olive oil, raisins, pepitas, almonds, salt, black pepper, chili flakes, and agave syrup.

5. Arrange on a baking sheet. Roast for 10 minutes, until soft.

TIP: To add a delicious crunch, try topping with the Roasted Pistachio Crumble (page 42).

1 pound sweet mini peppers
(bell peppers will work as well)

½ pound Fresno chilis
(fresh cayenne or serrano chilis
will work as well)

2 tablespoons minced garlic

2 tablespoons extra-virgin olive oil

2 tablespoons raisins

2 tablespoons pepitas

2 tablespoons sliced almonds

1 tablespoon sea salt

2 teaspoons black pepper

½ teaspoon red chili flakes

2 teaspoons agave syrup

TIP: If you live on the East Coast and can find Italian long hot peppers, replace both types of peppers in this recipe with 1½ to 2 pounds of the Italian long hots. Simply wash the whole peppers and toss them with the other ingredients before baking. This would be most similar to the dish I grew up eating!

TIP: The best part of this meal is taking a crunchy piece of Italian bread and soaking up all the juices the peppers were cooked in. This is one meal where nothing will go to waste.

GRILLED BROCCOLINI

SERVES 4 TO 6

This is one of the easiest and most satisfying vegetable dishes you can make. If you have the opportunity to follow through with the finished dish serving suggestions (see the tip below the recipe instructions), it can become so much more than a side dish. Earthy, hearty, sweet, and savory broccolini can be enjoyed as a full meal.

2 pounds, or 4 bunches, broccolini, washed

¼ cup extra-virgin olive oil

1 teaspoon minced garlic

1 teaspoon sea salt

1 teaspoon black pepper

Juice of ½ lemon (or as much as you like)

Vegan honey (optional)

TIP: If you can get your hands on one of the new vegan honeys on the market, drizzle some over the grilled broccolini to add a sweetness that will blow your mind! My own personal favorite vegan honey is the Mellody brand.

1 Preheat a grill to medium-high heat, approximately 400° to 450°F.

2 Bring a large pot of water to a boil. Add the broccolini and blanch it for 2 to 3 minutes. Shock it in ice water. Drain.

3 Chop at least 2 inches off the tough bottoms of the broccolini.

4 In a large bowl, combine the broccolini, olive oil, garlic, salt, and pepper.

5 Toss well to make sure all the broccolini is coated.

6 Place the broccolini directly on the grill and cook for 5 to 7 minutes, until charred and tender. Make sure to turn the broccolini a few times to get an even cook.

7 Transfer to a serving dish. Squeeze some lemon juice on the grilled broccolini and it is ready to serve. But there is so much more you can do to make this dish a star . . .

TIP: Grilled broccolini can be served by itself, as it's a wonderful green addition to any meal. However, if you are looking to expand on the horizon for your vegetables, serve this on warm Cashew Ricotta (page 33) topped with a little bit of Macadamia Parmigiano (page 35) or with Pangrattato (page 51) and a drizzle of homemade Chili Oil (page 52).

CALABRIAN PEPPERS *and* POTATOES

SERVES 4 TO 6

Known in Italy as *pipi e patati,* this is a slightly spicy Calabrian dish you can use as a side dish, a sandwich filling, on pasta, or with anything else you can think of. The perfect example of Calabrian cooking, it's so simple to make and it's so, so rich and delicious.

   To make this dish work well, it's important to use really good peppers. In Calabria, they like a distinctive type of flavorful pepper that unfortunately you can't find in the States. Instead, we use serrano peppers, Fresno peppers, Italian long hots, or any other spicy pepper that's got some flesh you can cook down to avoid a thick skin.

1 pound Yukon gold potatoes

1 pound (about 2) red bell peppers

½ pound (about 3) Calabrian peppers (or equivalent spicy pepper of choice)

¼ cup extra-virgin olive oil

1 cup yellow onion, sliced into thin strips

1 tablespoon smashed garlic cloves

2 teaspoons sea salt

2 teaspoons black pepper

1 teaspoon dried oregano

2 tablespoons filtered water

1 teaspoon Calabrian chili paste (optional)

4 to 5 fresh basil leaves, torn into pieces

Crusty toasted Italian bread, for serving

NOTE: I prefer Yukon gold, as they are very buttery and delicious on their own. If you can't find Yukons, try russets or small red potatoes.

1   Wash and slice the potatoes into ¼-inch-thick wedges. Slice the bell peppers into ¼-inch strips and remove the seeds. Chop the Calabrian peppers and remove the seeds if spice is not desired.

2   In a large sauté pan, heat the oil over medium heat. Add the potatoes and onion and cook for 10 to 12 minutes.

3   Add both of the peppers, the garlic, salt, black pepper, and oregano to the pan. Sauté for 5 minutes while stirring well.

4   Add the water to the pan. Cook, covered, for 10 minutes. The peppers and potatoes should be soft.

5   Remove from the heat and taste for salt and spice level. Add more salt if needed. If you desire a higher spice level, add the Calabrian chili paste and stir very well.

6   Sprinkle the basil on the peppers. Serve immediately with crusty toasted Italian bread.

CANDIED BRUSSELS SPROUTS

SERVES 4 TO 6

Like cauliflower and cabbage, brussels sprouts are a seasonal vegetable; they're best during fall or winter. And I do have a preference for organic brussels sprouts; they're smaller, juicier, and they just taste a whole lot better.

½ cup extra-virgin olive oil

½ cup maple syrup

1 tablespoon Dijon or stone-ground mustard

1 tablespoon roughly chopped shallots

1 teaspoon sea salt

1 teaspoon black pepper

1 pound brussels sprouts

1   Preheat the oven to 375°F.

2   Make the candy sauce by adding the olive oil, maple syrup, mustard, shallots, salt, and pepper to a high-speed blender. Blend until smooth, then set aside.

3   Prepare the brussels sprouts by removing the outer leaves and any brown spots. Cut off the stems as close to the bottoms of the sprouts as you can. If the sprouts are larger in size, cut them into halves or quarters. Be sure the pieces are all the same size, so they cook evenly. Wash thoroughly.

4   In a large mixing bowl, toss the prepared brussels sprouts with the candy sauce.

5   Spread the brussels sprouts, along with any extra sauce, on a large baking sheet and bake for 12 to 15 minutes. The brussels sprouts should be slightly crisp and browned around the edges, and you should be able to pierce them with a fork.

6   Serve immediately.

ROASTED HEIRLOOM CAULIFLOWER

SERVES 4 TO 6

I always like to cook heirloom cauliflowers because they're beautiful, with colors ranging from purple to green to orange. But if you can't find heirloom versions, your everyday white cauliflower will taste pretty much the same, just without the brilliant colors.

This roasted cauliflower is really a southern Italian/Sicilian-inspired dish with the addition of the pignoli and raisins (if you can find golden raisins, they will be extra special for this recipe). Roast these to your desired texture. Personally, I like them slightly crunchy.

---

1   Preheat the oven to 400°F.

2   In a large bowl, toss the cauliflower with the vegan butter, garlic, lemon juice, raisins, pignoli, salt, pepper, and paprika.

3   Spread the cauliflower on a baking sheet and roast for 10 to 15 minutes, until slightly crunchy.

4   Taste for salt. When you are ready to serve, sprinkle the parsley over the top.

5   Top with pistachio crumble.

4 cups heirloom cauliflower, washed and cut into 1-inch florets

¼ cup vegan butter, melted

2 teaspoons minced garlic

1½ teaspoons lemon juice

¼ cup raisins

¼ cup raw, unsalted pignoli (pine nuts)

1 teaspoon sea salt

1 teaspoon black pepper

½ teaspoon paprika

1 tablespoon chopped fresh parsley

Roasted Pistachio Crumble (page 42)

ROASTED LEMON ASPARAGUS

SERVES 4 TO 6

Simple and versatile, this lemon asparagus is excellent as a side dish or as an addition to Baked Ziti Alfredo on page 190. Asparagus is best when it's in season, which is spring in most areas of the country.

1 bunch asparagus, medium-sized

¼ cup extra-virgin olive oil

¼ cup lemon juice

2 teaspoons minced garlic

1 teaspoon sea salt

1 teaspoon black pepper

2 tablespoons Pangrattato (page 51)

Lemon slices

---

1   Preheat the oven to 350°F.

2   Wash the asparagus. Cut approximately 2 inches off the bottoms of the stalks.

3   In a large bowl, toss the asparagus in the olive oil, lemon juice, garlic, salt, and pepper.

4   Arrange on a baking sheet. Roast for 6 to 8 minutes. Cooking time will depend on the thickness of the asparagus. Do not overcook.

5   Top with the pangrattato and lemon slices.

TIP: You can also top your asparagus with Macadamia Parmigiano (page 35) for a more robust flavor. You can grill the asparagus, too!

STUFFED ARTICHOKES

SERVES 4 TO 6

Stuffed artichokes have always been a staple in my house. They make for the perfect dish, as each leaf is individually removed and enjoyed. Artichokes are quite a bit of work, but the experience is so worth it.

Most people have no idea how to cut, clean, prep, or eat artichokes. There is one part of the artichoke that is not edible: the choke, which is the hairy, spiny part deep inside. After you eat the outer leaves (well, you don't actually eat the leaves, you scrape them with your teeth) and just before you find the heart, you will get to the choke. You do not want to eat this part!

3 large artichokes

Juice of ½ lemon, plus
2 tablespoons

1 cup bread crumbs

¼ cup Macadamia
Parmigiano (page 35)

3 large garlic cloves, minced

1 tablespoon finely chopped shallot

¼ cup extra-virgin olive oil for
the bread crumb mix, plus more
for drizzling

¼ cup finely chopped fresh parsley

1 teaspoon sea salt, plus
more as needed

½ teaspoon black pepper

1 quart vegetable broth

2 cups filtered water

Maldon salt for topping

Toasted ciabatta, for serving

TIP: I use my Pangrattato recipe (page 51) for these stuffed artichokes. Feel free to use any Italian bread crumbs you like, making sure to read the ingredients first, as some store-bought bread crumbs contain milk or cheese.

1   Clean the artichokes: Cut the stem off the base of each artichoke. Reserve the stems to use in the stuffing. Remove the small outer leaves at the base, as they can be extremely tough.

2   Cut about ¾ inch off the top of the artichoke. Use kitchen scissors to cut the sharp tips off all the leaves. Rinse the artichokes under cool running water.

3   Prepare a bowl of lemon water (approximately 3 quarts of water with the juice of ½ lemon) to prevent the artichokes from oxidizing. Place each cleaned artichoke upside down in the lemon water and proceed to clean the other artichokes.

4   While the artichokes sit in the lemon water, make the stuffing.

5   Wash the artichoke stems. Peel, then dice them into very small pieces.

6   In a separate bowl, add the bread crumbs, chopped artichoke stems, macadamia parmigiano, garlic, shallots, the remaining lemon juice, the olive oil, parsley, salt, and pepper. Mix well.

Continued

7   In an oven-safe stockpot (large enough to hold the 3 artichokes), add the broth (I like to use Imagine No-Chicken Broth) and water. Heat over medium heat to bring the stock to a low boil.

8   Drain the artichokes on a kitchen towel or paper towels for 1 to 2 minutes to remove any excess water.

9   Place the artichokes stem-side down on a cutting board. With a small spoon and your fingers, nestle the bread crumb stuffing between the leaves. You can pull back the leaves with your fingers to add in the filling.

10 Add the stuffing in the middle and all throughout the leaves. Drizzle a tiny bit of olive oil and a pinch of sea salt on the tops of the stuffed artichokes.

11 Place the stuffed artichokes (stem-side down) in the stockpot with the simmering broth. Cover and cook for 40 to 45 minutes, or until the artichokes are fully cooked. (The cooking time really depends on the size of the artichokes.) You can add more water and a pinch of sea salt as the water cooks down, if needed. You know when the artichokes are fully cooked when you can easily pull off a leaf. If the leaf does not pull off easily, cover the pot and cook longer, until the artichokes are tender.

12 Turn on the oven broiler.

13 Once the artichokes are cooked, remove the lid from the pot. Place pot in the oven under the broiler and broil for 4 to 6 minutes, or until the artichokes are golden brown on top. If your pot doesn't fit under your broiler, transfer your artichokes to a smaller pan.

14 Remove the pot from the oven. Taste the broth for salt. Serve with all the broth and lots of toasted ciabatta. Depending on the size of the artichokes, more salt might be needed.

15 Drizzle with olive oil. Sprinkle with Maldon salt before serving.

16 To eat, pull a leaf off the artichoke and scrape the meat from the base of the leaf and stuffing using your teeth. Some leaves will be more tender than others. When you have removed all the green leaves, you will find light-colored leaves that are not meaty. These are hiding the part of the artichoke you cannot eat!

17 Take a small spoon and scoop out the middle of the artichokes. As you scoop, you will see the fuzzy part; make sure to remove it completely, as it's super spiny and not digestible. Once the choke is removed, the heart of the artichoke will appear.

18 This is where the toasted ciabatta bread comes in . . . use it to soak up all the juices as you eat the heart and clean your dish!

ROASTED WINTER VEGETABLES

SERVES 4 TO 6

Roasting is one of the easiest and most delicious ways to prepare vegetables. Even if you're a carnivore, you can still enjoy them and, of course, profit from all the necessary nutrients and wonderful flavors they offer.

2 to 3 pounds winter vegetables (such as squash, cauliflower, broccoli, brussels sprouts, Jerusalem artichokes, etc.)

3 to 5 garlic cloves

½ cup extra-virgin olive oil

1 tablespoon chopped fresh thyme leaves

1 tablespoon chopped fresh rosemary leaves

2 teaspoons sea salt

1 teaspoon black pepper

Pesto Calabrese (page 39), Gremolata (page 45), or Alfredo Sauce (page 44) for dipping (optional)

Pangrattato (page 51) and Macadamia Parmigiano (page 35), for topping (optional)

1   Preheat the oven to 425°F.

2   Wash the vegetables well. Cut them into similarly sized pieces so they cook evenly. Aim for 1-inch pieces for all root vegetables. Broccoli, cauliflower, and brussels sprouts can be larger. For example, brussels sprouts can be cut in half, broccoli cut into 1-inch florets.

3   Remove the skin from the garlic cloves and smash them. No need to chop; smashing the garlic will release its flavor.

4   Toss the vegetables with the garlic, olive oil, thyme, rosemary, salt, and pepper.

5   Spread them on a baking sheet and roast for 15 to 20 minutes. The high temperature will help the veggies brown and caramelize as they roast. The vegetables should be slightly crisp and browned around the edges and you should be able to pierce them with a fork.

6   Serve the roasted vegetables with one of the decadent sauces, such as pesto Calabrese or gremolata. Or dip the veggies into Alfredo sauce for a creamy and smooth finish. You can also enjoy the roasted vegetables topped with pangrattato and macadamia parmigiano.

TIP: For the best results, try roasting similar vegetables together. For example, all root vegetables will cook in around the same amount of time; likewise, all cruciferous vegetables will roast best together timing-wise.

GRILLED SUMMER VEGETABLES

SERVES 6 TO 8

No matter who you're entertaining—or even if you're just cooking for yourself or for your partner or family—you must have vegetables. And the best kind are seasonal, local, and organic ones. If you're lucky enough to have a nearby farmers market, support it, as you'll be helping not just your menu but also your local farmers. Summer vegetables are one reason why this is my absolute favorite time of the year. So simple yet so delicious.

2 zucchini

2 summer squash

2 bell peppers (any color except green)

1 bunch asparagus (1½ to 2 pounds)

12 green onions

¼ cup extra-virgin olive oil, plus more for drizzling (optional)

3 tablespoons aged balsamic vinegar

2 tablespoons chopped fresh parsley, plus more for garnish (optional)

1 teaspoon minced garlic

1 teaspoon sea salt

1 teaspoon black pepper

Basil leaves for garnish (optional)

Pinch of Maldon salt

TIP: These grilled vegetables are excellent if served with Gremolata (page 45), Pistachio Pesto (page 41); or Pesto Calabrese (page 39) and Roasted Pistachio Crumble (page 42).

1   Prepare the barbecue grill over medium-high heat or place a grill pan over medium-high heat.

2   Wash the zucchini and summer squash well. Cut off their ends, then chop them into ¼- to ½-inch-thick rectangles. Seed and halve the bell peppers. Wash the asparagus and break off the ends. Cut the roots off the green onions.

3   In a mixing bowl, combine the olive oil, vinegar, parsley, garlic, sea salt, and pepper. Whisk together well.

4   Brush all the vegetables with the oil mixture to coat lightly.

5   Grill the vegetables in batches until they are tender and lightly charred all over: 5 minutes for the asparagus and green onions; 7 minutes for the zucchini and squash; and 8 to 10 minutes for the bell peppers.

6   The key to getting those great grill marks is to not move the vegetables too frequently once they've been placed on the hot grill.

7   Arrange the vegetables on a platter and garnish with parsley, torn basil leaves, Maldon salt, and a drizzle of olive oil, if using.

SOUPS

Italian Wedding Soup, *Page 131*

PASTA E FAGIOLI

SERVES 6 TO 8

We called this "pasta fazool" and it was my childhood favorite, hands down. Grandma made it best, and Ma made it even better. This soup is comforting when it's chilly outside. I enjoy it anytime, as there is nothing more nostalgic.

1   In a large bowl, soak the borlotti beans overnight in water, covered. Drain.

2   In a stockpot, heat the olive oil over medium heat. Sauté the onion, celery, carrots, garlic, rosemary, thyme, oregano, paprika, pepper, and chili flakes, if using, for 10 to 12 minutes, until the onion is translucent.

3   Add the tomatoes, water, salt, and drained beans to the stockpot. Cover and simmer for 1 hour, or until the beans are fully cooked. Stir every 10 to 15 minutes as the beans cook.

4   Add the ditalini pasta to the stockpot and cook until al dente according to the directions on the package. Add salt if necessary.

5   Garnish with chopped parsley. Squeeze on some lemon juice and sprinkle with macadamia parmigiano, if using. Serve immediately.

NOTE: The pasta will thicken the broth a lot. This is intentional. This soup is honestly more like a stew—but Grandma would never have called it stew, so let's just move forward and eat! Leftover soup will last in the fridge for 4 to 5 days.

½ pound borlotti beans or cannellini beans

¼ cup extra-virgin olive oil

1 cup diced yellow onion

1 cup diced celery

1 cup diced carrots

2 tablespoons minced garlic

1 teaspoon chopped fresh rosemary leaves

1 teaspoon fresh thyme leaves

½ teaspoon dried oregano

½ teaspoon smoked paprika

½ teaspoon black pepper

Pinch of red chili flakes (optional)

1 cup mashed D.O.P. San Marzano whole peeled tomatoes

5 cups filtered water

1 tablespoon sea salt, plus more as needed

1 pound ditalini pasta (or other small pasta shape of your choice)

¼ cup chopped fresh parsley for garnish

Squeeze of lemon juice for serving (optional)

Macadamia Parmigiano for serving (page 35, optional)

MINESTRONE

SERVES 6 TO 8

Like many of the dishes from southern Italy, minestrone is naturally vegan. It's basically tomato soup loaded with lots of extra vegetables and beans. I have always felt it was one of the best foods to eat when you're feeling unwell, or if you just want to relax, because a good minestrone is very comforting.

1   In a stockpot, heat the olive oil over medium heat. Sauté the onion, celery, carrots, potatoes, garlic, oregano, thyme, and pepper for approximately 12 minutes, or until the onion is translucent.

2   Add the green beans, tomatoes, broth, water, and bay leaves. Bring to a boil, then lower the heat and simmer for 15 to 20 minutes.

3   Add the salt, chickpeas or cannellini beans, and spinach to the stockpot and bring to a boil again.

4   Remove the pot from the heat. Add the parsley and basil and remove the bay leaves.

5   Serve with a drizzle of olive oil and macadamia parmigiano sprinkled on top.

TIP: If you want a heartier soup, add in some small pasta, like ditalini.

2 tablespoons extra-virgin olive oil, plus more for drizzling

1 cup finely diced yellow onion

1 cup finely diced celery

1 cup finely diced carrots

1 cup finely diced Yukon gold potatoes

1 tablespoon minced garlic

1 teaspoon dried oregano

1 teaspoon dried thyme

½ teaspoon black pepper

1 cup green beans cut into 1-inch pieces (other veggies can be used instead)

1½ cups mashed D.O.P. San Marzano tomatoes

2 cups vegetable broth

2 cups filtered water

2 bay leaves

2 teaspoons sea salt

1 cup cooked chickpeas or cannellini beans (canned are okay)

1 cup baby spinach

½ cup chopped fresh parsley

½ cup chopped fresh basil

Macadamia Parmigiano (page 35) for serving

GIAMBOTTA

SERVES 6 TO 8

It's funny how so much of what my family ate when I was a child was actually already vegan, such as pasta e fagioli and this recipe for giambotta, a summery vegetable stew that comes from my grandmother's hometown of Calabria.

If you do not have chickpeas, it's okay to use cannellini beans—or none at all! The purpose of this recipe is to use whatever vegetables are in season, or to use extra vegetables you have on hand, so feel free to play with the vegetable list and customize this to your liking!

---

1 Heat the olive oil in a stockpot over medium heat. Sauté the onion, celery, carrots, garlic, thyme, tarragon, and red chili flakes for 8 to 10 minutes, until the onion is translucent.

2 Add the diced potatoes and sauté for approximately 5 minutes.

3 Add the eggplant and red bell peppers and sauté for 2 to 3 minutes.

4 Add the tomatoes, bay leaves, and parsley and cook at a low boil for 12 to 15 minutes.

5 Add the cooked chickpeas, zucchini, salt, and pepper and continue to cook for approximately 5 minutes. The vegetables should be firm, not mushy.

6 Remove from the heat. Remove the bay leaves and add the basil.

TIP: This soup is best served with toasted ciabatta bread!

¼ cup extra-virgin olive oil

2 cups diced yellow onion

1 cup diced celery

1 cup diced carrots

2 tablespoons very thinly sliced garlic

1 tablespoon fresh thyme leaves

1 tablespoon fresh tarragon leaves

¼ teaspoon red chili flakes

2 cups medium-diced Yukon gold potatoes

1 cup peeled and diced eggplant

1 cup diced red bell peppers

28-ounce can whole peeled D.O.P. tomatoes, mashed

2 bay leaves

¼ cup chopped fresh parsley, stems included

1 cup cooked chickpeas (canned and drained are okay)

1 cup diced zucchini

1½ teaspoons sea salt

1½ teaspoons black pepper

¼ cup fresh basil leaves, torn into small pieces

ESCAROLE *and* BEANS

SERVES 6 TO 8

Escarole is a bitter, green leafy vegetable that few Americans are familiar with. But in southern Italy, this is a staple vegetable used in multiple dishes. Escarole and beans is another naturally vegan soup. You can make this as a soup or as a stew, depending on how much water you use. And just because it's so simple doesn't mean that it isn't delicious, so you have to make sure you have lots of bread handy because you'll be cleaning your bowl down to the last drop.

¼ cup extra-virgin olive oil

2 cups finely diced yellow onion

2 cups finely diced celery

2 tablespoons minced garlic

2 teaspoons smoked paprika

2 teaspoons chopped fresh thyme leaves

½ teaspoon chili flakes

3 heads of escarole

2 cups vegetable broth

2 cups filtered water

2 bay leaves

2 cups precooked (or canned) cannellini beans

2 teaspoons sea salt

2 teaspoons black pepper

1   Add the olive oil, onion, celery, garlic, smoked paprika, thyme, and chili flakes to a stockpot. Cook over medium heat until the onion and celery are soft, 10 to 12 minutes.

2   Wash and chop the escarole. Add it to the pot and cook for 3 to 5 minutes.

3   Add the broth, water, and bay leaves and bring to a boil.

4   Add the precooked cannellini beans, salt, and pepper. Taste and adjust the salt and pepper as needed. Remove the bay leaves.

TIP: This soup is best served with toasted ciabatta bread!

BUTTERNUT SQUASH BISQUE

SERVES 6 TO 8

This soup is a tradition for fall and winter holidays. You are guaranteed to impress your friends and family on Thanksgiving with this homemade comfort soup.

---

1   In a stockpot, heat the olive oil over medium heat. Sauté the onion, carrots, celery, garlic, and ginger for 10 minutes.

2   Add the butternut squash and coconut milk to the pot and stir.

3   Cover the pot and bring the soup to a boil over medium-high heat. Decrease the heat to medium-low.

4   Keep the pot covered and simmer the soup, stirring occasionally for 30 minutes, or until the squash is tender.

5   Stir in the water, maple syrup, orange zest, salt, pepper, cinnamon, and nutmeg.

6   Use an immersion blender to blend the soup until it has a smooth, creamy consistency. This soup should not be porridge-like—add more water if the soup is too thick.

7   Garnish with green onions, parsley, spiced pepitas, and a drizzle of olive oil.

2 tablespoons extra-virgin olive oil, plus more for drizzling

3 cups diced onion

3 cups diced carrots

3 cups diced celery

¼ cup peeled and diced fresh ginger

8 cups peeled and cubed butternut squash

6 cups coconut milk

1½ cups filtered water

2 tablespoons maple syrup

2 tablespoons grated orange zest

1 teaspoon sea salt

¼ tsp black pepper

1 teaspoon cinnamon

1 teaspoon ground nutmeg

¼ cup thinly sliced green onions for topping

¼ cup chopped fresh parsley for topping

2 tablespoons Spiced Pepitas (page 57) for topping

ITALIAN WEDDING SOUP

SERVES 6 TO 8

Italian wedding soup is one of the more fun soups my family used to make when I was a kid. It's an odd name that actually comes from a mistranslation of the Italian phrase *minestra maritata* ("married soup"). *Minestra maritata* more directly translates to "wedded broths." So it's broths rather than people that are getting married. Also, I can tell you I've been to countless cousins' weddings and nobody ever served it.

Wedding soup is a vegetable soup, similar to a minestrone, but it always contains pastina, which are tiny little pastas, and tiny meatballs (see page 69 for the recipe for polpettine), which means that kids love it! Here, you make the meatballs teaspoon-size and roll them up good and tight. Bake them and set them aside to add to the soup.

---

1 Preheat the oven to 350°F.

2 Cook the pasta in a pot of boiling salted water until al dente. Drain, then rinse under cool water. Set aside.

3 Use a teaspoon to portion the polpettine base into small balls. Then roll them between your palms into compact balls.

4 Oil a baking sheet. Arrange the meatballs on it, then bake for 12 to 14 minutes, flipping halfway through.

5 In a stockpot, heat the olive oil over medium heat. Sauté the onion, celery, carrots, potato, garlic, rosemary, thyme, oregano, smoked paprika, pepper, and salt for 12 to 15 minutes.

6 Add the water and bay leaves and bring to a boil. Boil for 8 to 10 minutes.

7 Add the lemon juice and escarole (or spinach), bring back to boil, and cook for 5 to 7 minutes.

8 Add the baked meatballs and cooked acini di pepe pasta. Bring back to a boil. Once boiling, remove from the heat. Taste for salt.

9 Garnish with olive oil (or chili oil, if using) and Maldon salt.

½ pound acini di pepe pasta (or any pastina, such as ditalini or orzo)

½ cup Polpettine base (page 69). Stop after step 6, before forming into balls

2 tablespoons extra-virgin olive oil, plus more for drizzling

1 cup diced yellow onion

1 cup diced celery

1 cup diced carrots

1 cup diced Yukon gold potato

1 tablespoon minced garlic

1 teaspoon chopped fresh rosemary leaves

1 teaspoon chopped fresh thyme leaves

1 teaspoon dried oregano

1 teaspoon smoked paprika

1 teaspoon black pepper

1 tablespoon sea salt

4 cups filtered water

2 bay leaves

1 tablespoon lemon juice

2 cups chopped escarole, or fresh spinach

Chili Oil (page 52, optional) for drizzling

Maldon salt

SICILIAN RED LENTIL SOUP

SERVES 6 TO 8

Lentils are a staple in Italy. In my cabinet I like to keep all different types: green, brown, black, red, and Umbrian—and there are so many different ways to make soup out of them.

I have two favorite soups: a Sicilian red lentil soup and an Umbrian Lentil Soup (page 133). The Sicilian red lentil soup is a southern Italian offering (although somewhat influenced by Northern African cuisine), and it's very lemony and fresh, unlike most other lentil soups.

---

1   In a stockpot, heat the olive oil over medium heat. Sauté the onion, carrots, and celery for approximately 10 minutes.

2   Lower the heat to low, add the garlic, cumin, coriander, smoked paprika, and chili flakes, and sauté for another 5 minutes.

3   Add the water and lentils and increase the heat. Bring to a boil, then lower the heat and simmer until the lentils are fully cooked, 20 to 25 minutes.

4   Remove from the heat and blend with an immersion blender. The soup should be textured rather than completely smooth.

5   Add the salt, pepper, and lemon juice and stir well. Add more salt if necessary.

6   Garnish with a drizzle of olive oil and a generous sprinkle of parsley. Add a pinch of smoked paprika, if using.

2 tablespoons extra-virgin olive oil, plus more for drizzling

3 cups diced onion

2 cups diced carrots

1 cup diced celery

2 tablespoons minced garlic

2 teaspoons ground cumin

2 teaspoons ground coriander

2 teaspoons smoked paprika, plus more for topping (optional)

¼ pinch chili flakes

16 cups filtered water

4 cups dry red lentils, rinsed

1 tablespoon sea salt

1 teaspoon black pepper

1½ cups lemon juice

¼ cup chopped parsley, plus more for topping

UMBRIAN LENTIL SOUP

SERVES 6 TO 8

This is my other favorite lentil soup, which differs from the Sicilian Red Lentil Soup because Umbrian lentils, unlike green lentils, cannot be overcooked; you can forget that you left the soup on the stove, walk away, take a shower—no matter, the lentils will still keep their texture, their shape, and their bite. You can make a huge pot of soup and leave it sitting on the stove, and it'll be exactly the way it was the first time you ate it as well as the fifth time. You can even freeze it and defrost it a month later and it still holds up.

- 2 tablespoons extra-virgin olive oil
- 2 cups diced yellow onion
- 1 cup diced celery
- 1 cup diced carrot
- 2 tablespoons minced garlic
- 2 teaspoons sea salt, plus more if needed
- 2 teaspoons black pepper
- 2 teaspoons chopped fresh thyme leaves
- 1 teaspoon dried oregano
- 1 teaspoon smoked paprika
- 1 pinch of chili flakes (optional)
- 2 cups filtered water, plus more if needed
- 4 cups vegetable broth
- 3 bay leaves
- 2 cups dry Umbrian lentils
- 2 cups baby spinach
- ¼ bunch parsley, chopped, for topping

1 In a stockpot, heat the olive oil over medium heat. Sauté the onion, celery, carrot, garlic, salt, pepper, thyme, oregano, paprika, and chili flakes (if using) for 12 minutes, or until the onion is translucent.

2 Add the water, broth, bay leaves, and lentils. Bring to a boil, then lower the heat and cook for 20 to 25 minutes, or until the lentils are fully cooked. Add more water if needed.

3 Add the baby spinach and simmer for 5 more minutes. Remove from the heat. Remove the bay leaves. Add more salt if necessary.

4 Top with the parsley.

ROASTED GARLIC CREAMY TOMATO SOUP

SERVES 6 TO 8

There's nothing like hot, creamy tomato soup along with some crunchy ciabatta to clean the bottom of your bowl. This soup is guaranteed to comfort you like a warm blanket on a cold day.

1   In a stockpot, heat the olive oil over medium heat. Sauté the onion and carrots for 10 to 12 minutes, or until the onion and carrots are soft.

2   Add the garlic and simmer for another 3 minutes.

3   Add the tomatoes and bay leaves. Bring to a low boil, then lower the heat and simmer for 45 minutes.

4   Add the cashew cream, smoked paprika, salt, and pepper. Return to a simmer and simmer for 15 minutes.

5   Add the roasted garlic. Remove the pot from the heat. Remove the bay leaves.

6   Using an immersion blender, blend until smooth and strain through a chinois. If you don't have an immersion blender, a regular one will do.

7   If desired, serve topped with microgreens, freshly ground pepper, and a drizzle of olive oil.

2 tablespoons extra-virgin olive oil, plus extra for drizzling (optional)

2 cups diced yellow onion

1 cup diced carrots

2 tablespoons minced garlic

7 cups D.O.P. San Marzano tomatoes (approximately two 28-ounce cans)

2 bay leaves

1 cup Cashew Cream (page 56)

1 tablespoon smoked paprika

1 tablespoon sea salt

1 teaspoon black pepper, plus extra for serving (optional)

¼ cup Roasted Garlic (page 46)

Microgreens for serving (optional)

PASTA

FRESH PASTA

SERVES 4 TO 6

I absolutely love the organic dried pastas made in Italy, bronze-extruded to perfection.

However, there are certain types of pasta that are simply more fun (and more delicious) to make fresh. I truly believe that fresh pasta might be the most wonderful thing that you can ever make, especially when you realize how simple it is to create. You don't even need a pasta machine; but if you do have one, you'll have many more options for shapes. If you do not have a pasta machine, you can roll your pasta with a rolling pin. But, if you don't even have a rolling pin, you can rough it like my grandma and use a wine bottle!

If this is your first time, it might seem intimidating to make fresh pasta. I promise you, this will blow your mind once you do it yourself!

675 grams semolina flour

75 grams pasta double zero flour (aka 00 flour or pasta fresca), plus more for dusting

350 grams filtered water

38 grams extra-virgin olive oil

12 grams sea salt

NOTE: This recipe makes 1,135 grams of fresh pasta, which is 2½ pounds.

I've given the ingredient measurements in grams. When you're making pasta or bread of any kind, it's really a science, so you should get right down to the exact amounts for the recipe.

---

1   On a large, clean work surface (preferably wood), pour the semolina and double zero flours into one pile. Make a well in the top.

2   Little by little, slowly add the water, olive oil, and salt into the center of the well. Use your hands to fold in the flours slowly from the edges to the middle to form a dough, being careful not to allow the liquid to spill out.

3   Knead the dough until firm but not too sticky.

4   Place the dough ball in a bowl, cover with a damp cloth, and let it rest for 30 minutes.

5   Cut the dough ball into quarters.

6   Roll out each quarter of the dough by hand with a rolling pin and shape by hand, as follows, or use a pasta machine.

Continued

ROLLING PASTA BY HAND

Rolling your own pasta by hand can feel very rewarding.

1   Dust the work surface with flour and then dust the dough balls with flour.

2   Place your rolling pin in the center of a dough ball. Push the rolling pin outward. Turn the dough one quarter and repeat, until the dough is evenly thinned out. Roll the dough to approximately 1/16 inch thick (or as thin as you can get it). You should be able to see the color of your hand underneath the dough. Repeat for each dough ball.

SHAPE THE PASTA

FOR LASAGNA

Cut the rolled-out dough into approximately 3 by 5-inch strips. It's not super important to follow an exact size, but it is important to keep the size uniform.

FOR TAGLIATELLE

Cut the rolled-out pasta dough in half. Position one half of dough in front of you and, starting at the end closest, begin to roll the dough into a loose tube. Cut off the uneven ends. Using a sharp knife, cut the tube across into strands (approximately 1/4 inch wide). Uncurl the strands and swirl them together into a nest. Set aside until you are ready to cook. Repeat with the rest of the dough.

FOR PAPPARDELLE

Following the instructions for the tagliatelle, perform the exact same technique, except cut the strands wider into 3/4 inch to just over 1 inch wide.

Continued

FOR CAVATELLI

Roll a portion of the dough ball into a long rope. Cut the rope crosswise into ½-inch pieces. Using two fingers, press and roll each piece of dough until it curves over itself. This will create the curl in the pasta. You can also roll the pieces of pasta against a fork (like Fresh Gnocchi, page 148) or use a cavatelli board if you have one.

PASTA MACHINE INSTRUCTIONS

Cut the dough into 4 pieces. Run each dough piece through your pasta machine roller, beginning on the thickest setting and repeating on successively thinner settings until you reach your desired thickness.

FOR LASAGNA

Cut the pasta sheet into strips long enough to fit your baking pan. Assemble the lasagna as instructed on page 155. You do not need to cook the pasta in advance. The pasta will cook as it bakes.

FOR TAGLIATELLE

Cut the pasta sheet into 12-inch-long pieces. Position the sheet in front of you and, starting at the end closest, begin to roll the dough into a loose tube. Using a sharp knife, cut each tube across into strands (approximately ¼ inch wide). Uncurl the strands, swirl them together into a nest, and set them aside until you are ready to cook.

FOR PAPPARDELLE

Following the instructions for the tagliatelle, perform the same technique but cut the strands wider, ¾ to 1 inch wide.

PASTA POMODORO

SERVES 2 TO 4

Let's talk about tomato sauce. I have two different versions: the first is Marinara Sauce (page 37), which is a warm and wonderful slow-cooked sauce that has spices, fresh garlic, olive oil, and basil.

Pomodoro, however, is not really a sauce. It is composed of fresh cherry tomatoes seeded and cut into small pieces that are simply cooked down with garlic and oil. Pasta pomodoro is really just a hearty, chunky tomato dish. When you're making the pasta, you can get a little fancy and put a bit of marinara sauce in the pan with the tomatoes and mix it together a little bit—as you'll see in this recipe. This combination of pomodoro and marinara is my favorite.

2 tablespoons extra-virgin olive oil

1 teaspoon minced garlic

1 cup halved cherry tomatoes

Pinch of sea salt, plus 2 tablespoons for the pasta water

Pinch of black pepper

2 cups Marinara Sauce (page 37)

1 pound pasta (spaghetti, penne, or rigatoni—almost any shape goes well in pomodoro)

Cashew Ricotta (page 33), for topping

Chopped fresh basil, for topping

1   In a large pot, bring 4 to 6 quarts of water to a rolling boil.

2   Meanwhile, heat the olive oil in a large sauté pan over medium-low heat. Sauté the garlic, cherry tomatoes, pinch of salt, and pepper for 4 to 5 minutes.

3   Add the marinara sauce and continue to sauté over medium-low heat.

4   Add the remaining 2 tablespoons of salt to the boiling water. Add the pasta and cook until very al dente, a little more than half the recommended cooking time.

5   Use pasta tongs to transfer the pasta to the sauté pan and add ½ cup of the pasta cooking water.

6   Continue to cook the pasta in the sauce, tossing around the pasta until it absorbs all the water and is perfectly al dente. Check to make sure the pasta does not overcook. Add more pasta water if needed. The sauce should stay juicy!

7   Serve topped with cashew ricotta and basil.

FRESH RAVIOLI

SERVES 4 TO 6

Ravioli are filled pasta pillows that can be made in assorted shapes and sizes: square, round, half-moons. Personally, I don't care what shape the ravioli is…I love them all! The experience of biting into these pockets of pasta, created by hand and bursting with love, is what makes them so special.

Instead of cutting the fresh pasta dough into shapes, you use the lasagna sheets. For ravioli, it's best to use a pasta machine so the sheets are of uniform thickness. Three classic ravioli fillings are Almond Ricotta (page 33), Cashew Ricotta (page 33), and Spinach Ricotta (page 153).

Once you make these ravioli a few times and feel confident, consider playing with other filling possibilities, such as adding artichoke or squash to the ricotta.

675 grams semolina flour

75 grams double zero flour (aka 00 flour or pasta fresca), plus more for dusting

350 grams filtered water

38 grams extra-virgin olive oil

12 grams sea salt

4 cups vegan ricotta

---

1   Follow the instructions to make the pasta sheets for lasagna (page 141). Make sure to cut them into equal lengths so they can match up end to end.

2   Lay one of the pasta sheets on your clean work surface.

3   Using your fingers and a spoon, place approximately ¾ tablespoon of filling ½ inch from the edge of one of the long sides of the dough sheet. Repeat every inch for a total of approximately 6 dollops down the length of the sheet.

4   Spray the pasta sheet with a light mist of water. This will help the two layers stick together. Fold the sheet in half lengthwise and press the two edges together. Press between each dollop of filling to seal.

5   Use a ravioli wheel (or a sharp knife) to cut the ravioli into 2-inch squares.

TIP: If you do not have a ravioli wheel and you are using a knife, take a fork and press the tines on all the edges of each individual ravioli. This will help seal it tighter and also prevent it from breaking open during cooking. If you want round ravioli, use the rim of a glass or something else that's round, such as a cookie cutter.

6   If you do not plan to eat the uncooked ravioli right away, dust them with extra flour and freeze in an airtight freezer container or bag. They will keep for 3 to 6 months.

7   To cook the ravioli, bring a large pot of salted water to a rolling boil. Add the ravioli. Cook for 2½ to 3 minutes. Once the ravioli float to the top, they are done. Use a slotted spoon to take them out.

TIP: My recipe for Ravioli Pomodoro is on the next page, but that is simply one example. You can also try topping your ravioli with one of the pestos (pages 38–41), the Cacio e Pepe sauce (page 161), making it alla vodka (see Penne alla Vodka, page 181)—or, if you are feeling super fancy or really want to make an impression, make a truffle cream by adding fresh truffle to the Alfredo Sauce (page 44)!

> Ravioli are an extremely important part of Italian cuisine. They are often prepared with loved ones for Christmas feasts, or other big family celebrations such as birthdays and anniversaries.

RAVIOLI POMODORO

SERVES 2 TO 4

There really is nothing as comforting as these fluffy little pillows of pasta stuffed with your favorite plant-based cheese. As a kid, the food I looked forward to the most was ravioli. My very favorite part was that my mom couldn't wrap her head around how many to make, so she always made enough for an army— which meant leftovers! The next morning, I would wake up and go downstairs and eat the ice-cold ravioli that were stuck together with Mom's delicious sauce. So, make more than enough!

2 tablespoons extra-virgin olive oil

½ cup halved cherry or grape tomatoes

Pinch of sea salt, plus 2 tablespoons for the pasta water

Pinch of black pepper

2 cups Marinara Sauce (page 37)

1 pound Fresh Ravioli (page 144)

½ cup melted Cashew Mozzarella (page 34, optional)

Basil leaves

Macadamia Parmigiano (page 35, optional)

Chili Oil (page 52, optional)

1 In a large pot, bring 4 to 6 quarts of water to a rolling boil.

2 Meanwhile, heat the olive oil in a large sauté pan over medium-low heat. Add the cherry tomatoes, pinch of salt, and pepper and sauté for 2 minutes.

3 Add the marinara sauce and continue to sauté over medium-low heat.

4 While the sauce is cooking, add the remaining 2 tablespoons of salt to the boiling water. Add the ravioli and cook until they float to the top of the water, 3 to 5 minutes. They should be al dente.

5 Use a slotted spoon to transfer the ravioli to the sauté pan and add ¼ cup of the pasta cooking water. Cook the ravioli in the sauce, very gently tossing them around. Make sure the ravioli do not overcook or break apart.

6 Add the melted mozzarella, if using, and transfer to a serving bowl.

7 Garnish with freshly torn basil; add a sprinkle of macadamia parmigiano and some chili oil, if using.

FRESH GNOCCHI

SERVES 4 TO 6

I love gnocchi, a magical combination of two of my favorite food groups: pasta and potatoes. You just put them together to make one perfect little pillow that you can drown in sauce and mozzarella to serve alla Sorrentina (page 150) and then stuff in your mouth, one after the next. Heaven.

2 pounds Yukon gold potatoes, washed

2 cups double zero flour (aka 00 flour or pasta fresca), plus more for dusting

¼ cup extra-virgin olive oil

2 teaspoons sea salt, plus 2 tablespoons for the gnocchi cooking water

½ teaspoon black pepper

---

1   Submerge the potatoes in a medium pot filled with cold water. Bring the water to a boil. Reduce the heat to medium-low and simmer for approximately 45 minutes, or until the potatoes are fully cooked and easily pierced with a fork.

2   Drain the potatoes, allow them to cool completely, and then peel off the skin with your fingers. It should slide right off.

3   Pass the potatoes through a potato ricer.

4   Transfer the potatoes to a clean work surface, preferably wood, such as a large wooden cutting board. Sprinkle the flour over the potatoes.

5   Gently begin to fold the potatoes and flour together using your hands. Once the flour is mostly mixed together with the potatoes, use your fingers to make a well in the center of the dough.

6   In a separate bowl or glass, mix the olive oil, salt, and pepper together.

7   Pour the olive oil mixture into the well in the dough.

8   Using your hands, gradually combine the potato mixture with the olive oil until all the oil is incorporated. Knead gently until there are no dry bits of flour remaining. Try not to overknead the dough, as that will make it tough.

9   Now you are ready to roll! Using a sharp knife or a dough scraper, divide the dough into 8 pieces. Roll each piece into a ¾- to 1-inch-thick strip. Cut each strip into ¾- to 1-inch pieces. Try to ensure each piece is the same size and do not go larger than 1 inch. This is the perfect size.

10 Roll each piece of gnocchi over a floured gnocchi paddle (or simply use a fork) to create the ridges.

11 Cook immediately or transfer to a parchment-lined baking sheet dusted with flour, keeping the gnocchi in a single layer to prevent sticking.

TO COOK THE GNOCCHI

1   In a large pot, bring 4 to 6 quarts of water to a boil. Add the remaining 2 tablespoons of salt. Boil the gnocchi in batches for 2 to 2½ minutes each, until they float to the top of the water. Have your sauté pan ready if you plan to make Gnocchi alla Sorrentina (page 150).

2   Alternatively, if you do not plan to cook the gnocchi right away, line a baking sheet with parchment paper. Place the gnocchi in a single layer on the sheet, cover it with plastic wrap, and place it in the freezer for 1 hour. Then uncover, transfer the gnocchi into a freezer bag, and return to the freezer. These will last frozen for about 2 months. When you are ready to cook them, thaw at room temperature for 20 to 30 minutes.

TIP: Gnocchi should be light and fluffy, with little grooves that love to hold your favorite sauces. Don't skip the step of making those ridges. You will love them when you see all the sauce they grab!

GNOCCHI *alla* SORRENTINA

SERVES 2 TO 4

Gnocchi are fluffy little clouds of pasta and potato. They're simple to prepare, filling, delicious, and inexpensive, so there's no excuse not to make them.

The custom in Italy is to eat gnocchi on Thursdays. I'm not really sure why, but sometimes it's best to not ask questions, just stick to the traditions, because I can't think of a better one. Every Thursday should be Gnocchi Thursday.

This gnocchi recipe for alla Sorrentina is my favorite way to eat gnocchi, but once you make them and you feel comfortable, I urge you to try some of other sauces listed in this book. Gnocchi can go with virtually any of them. So play, have fun, and share with friends, family, and neighbors—you'll make new friends if you share with strangers.

2 tablespoons extra-virgin olive oil

Pinch of sea salt, plus 2 tablespoons for the pasta water

Pinch of black pepper

2 cups Marinara Sauce (page 37)

1 pound Fresh Gnocchi (page 148)

½ cup melted Cashew Mozzarella (page 34)

Fresh basil leaves

Macadamia Parmigiano (page 35, optional)

1   In a large pot, bring 4 to 6 quarts of water to a rolling boil.

2   Meanwhile, heat the olive oil with the pinch of salt and pepper in a large sauté pan over medium-low heat for 2 minutes. Add the marinara sauce and continue to cook over medium-low heat.

3   Once the water has reached a rolling boil, add the remaining 2 tablespoons of salt. Add the gnocchi and cook for 2 to 2½ minutes, or until the gnocchi float to the top of the water.

4   Use a slotted spoon to transfer the pasta to the sauté pan and add ¼ cup of the pasta water. Cook the gnocchi in the sauce, tossing them around. Make sure they do not overcook.

5   Add the melted mozzarella and transfer to a serving bowl.

6   Garnish with freshly torn basil and a sprinkle of macadamia parmigiano, if using.

SPINACH RICOTTA CANNELLONI

SERVES 4 TO 6

Cannelloni was another one of those dinners that I couldn't wait for my mom to make. I think it's the excitement of cutting into a pocket of pasta that's just bursting at the seams with delicious homemade plant-based cheeses. The surprise of the blended textures, the softness of the cheese and the pasta and the sauce and everything else that happens just takes away all your problems. It's basically food as therapy.

SPINACH RICOTTA

1   Soak the cashews in water for a minimum of 4 hours. Drain and rinse well before using.

2   Place the cashews, olive oil, water, garlic, vinegar, yeast, salt, pepper, whole baby spinach, and tofu in a high-speed blender and blend until smooth. Taste for salt. Add more if desired.

3   Fold in the chopped baby spinach.

CANNELLONI

1   Fill a disposable pastry bag with the spinach ricotta and tape the large open end tightly closed. Cut the pointy tip off the bag. (If you don't have a pastry bag, you can use a plastic ziplock bag, carefully cutting off the tip of a corner of the bag.)

2   Hold a cannelloni shell in one hand. Insert the pastry bag into the middle of the shell. Slowly squeeze the pastry bag to fill the pasta shell from the middle out. Turn the shell around and repeat the same from the other side. This will ensure the entire pasta shell is filled completely with the ricotta.

Continued

SPINACH RICOTTA

2 cups raw, unsalted cashews

1 cup extra-virgin olive oil

½ cup filtered water

2 tablespoons minced garlic

2 tablespoons apple cider vinegar

2 tablespoons nutritional yeast

1 tablespoon sea salt

2 teaspoons black pepper

1 cup whole baby spinach

14 ounces (1 package) extra firm tofu, broken into pieces

1 cup chopped baby spinach

CANNELLONI

About 16 dry cannelloni shells

8 cups Marinara Sauce (page 37), plus more if desired

1 cup Cashew Mozzarella (page 34), plus more if desired

Torn fresh basil leaves for topping

Macadamia Parmigiano (page 35, optional)

3   Preheat the oven to 375°F.

4   Coat the bottom of a 9 x 13-inch baking pan with approximately 2 cups of the marinara sauce.

5   Place as many of the stuffed cannelloni shells in the pan as can fit so there are no large gaps between them.

6   Pour 2 to 3 cups of the remaining marinara sauce on the shells, making sure to cover every bit of them with sauce. This may seem like an excessive amount of sauce, but the pasta will cook in the sauce. If you do not use enough sauce, the cannelloni can be crunchy or burned.

7   Drizzle the cashew mozzarella over the top. (Use more if desired. I can never get enough!)

8   Cover the baking pan with foil. Bake in the oven for approximately 20 minutes.

9   Remove the foil and bake for another 10 minutes. Test to make sure the pasta is cooked to perfection.

10 Remove from the oven. Let the cannelloni rest for 3 to 4 minutes before serving.

11 Serve with extra sauce and freshly torn basil. Top with macadamia parmigiano, if using.

LASAGNA PURA

SERVES 9 TO 12

My grandmother and my mother always cooked up the best lasagna imaginable, and the cheese was an important part of it. So when I went vegan, I was determined to create a lasagna that was just as good—without the animal products. I tried so many different versions and didn't nail it until after I graduated from college. Every time I tried a different version, my parents would bravely taste, only to shake their heads. My mother was polite, but my father would simply say "no."

It wasn't until I finally came up with the Cashew Ricotta recipe (page 33) that the lasagna passed the Punzone test.

CREMINI MUSHROOM "MEAT"

1 Preheat the oven to 350°F.

2 Combine the mushrooms, olive oil, garlic, salt, and pepper in a mixing bowl.

3 Spread the mushrooms on a baking sheet. Roast them for 10 minutes.

4 Remove the mushrooms from the oven, add the nutritional yeast and parsley, and mix. Let cool.

LASAGNA

1 Increase the oven temperature to 375°F.

2 In a 9 by 13-inch baking pan, spread 1 cup of marinara sauce.

3 Place 6 lasagna noodles in a single layer on the sauce. Spread ½ cup of the marinara sauce over the lasagna noodles. Top with five 4-ounce scoops of cashew ricotta (2½ cups total). Spread 2 cups of the baby spinach over the ricotta.

Continued

CREMINI MUSHROOM "MEAT"

8 cups cleaned, sliced cremini mushrooms (approximately 1 pound)

2 tablespoons extra-virgin olive oil

3 tablespoons minced garlic

1 tablespoon sea salt

2 teaspoons black pepper

2 tablespoons nutritional yeast

½ cup minced fresh parsley (approximately ½ bunch with bottom of the stems removed)

LASAGNA

4½ cups Marinara Sauce (page 37) for building the lasagna, plus another 5 cups for serving

5 cups Cashew Ricotta (page 33)

18 lasagna noodles (page 141)

4 cups baby spinach

3 cups Cremini Mushroom "Meat" (recipe above)

9 tablespoons firm Cashew Mozzarella (page 34)

4 Add another layer of 6 lasagna noodles. Pour on 1 cup of the remaining marinara sauce. Spread on five more 4-ounce scoops of cashew ricotta (2½ cups total). Sprinkle with the cremini mushroom "meat." Spread on the remaining 2 cups of the baby spinach. Pour on 1 cup of the remaining marinara sauce.

5 Add another layer of 6 lasagna noodles. Pour on 1 more cup of the marinara sauce. Spoon on the cashew mozzarella, in three rows of 3 tablespoons.

6 Now that you've built it, you bake it. Cover the baking pan with foil and bake for 50 minutes.

7 Remove the foil and let it cool for 10 minutes before cutting.

8 Cut the lasagna into 9 or 12 squares (depending on how hungry your guests are!). Serve with the remaining marinara sauce to pour over each portion.

SPAGHETTI AGLIO, OLIO E PEPERONCINO

SERVES 2 TO 4

This dish is brilliant in both its taste and simplicity. Use the best extra-virgin olive oil you can find—each strand of spaghetti should be glistening with olive oil. When it's done perfectly, the oil will glaze your lips and drip down to your chin with each bite.

¾ cup extra-virgin olive oil

4 garlic cloves, sliced razor thin or minced

2 fresh Calabrian chili peppers (or cayenne peppers), sliced into ⅛-inch-thick rounds

½ cup chopped fresh parsley, plus more for topping

1 teaspoon sea salt, plus 2 tablespoons for the pasta water

1 pound spaghetti

Pangrattato (page 51) for topping

Maldon salt for topping

1   In a large pot, bring 4 to 6 quarts of water to a rolling boil.

2   Meanwhile, in a deep sauté pan, heat ½ cup of the olive oil over medium to low heat. Sauté the garlic, chili peppers, parsley, and 1 teaspoon of the salt. Add 1 tablespoon of olive oil every minute or two until you've added it all. Cook slowly until the garlic starts to sizzle, but do not let the garlic burn.

3   Lower the heat all the way down so it stops cooking before you add the pasta.

4   Add the remaining 2 tablespoons of salt to the boiling water. Add the spaghetti and cook until it's barely al dente, a little more than half the recommended cooking time.

5   Remove the spaghetti from the boiling water and add it to the sauté pan along with 2 cups of the pasta cooking water.

6   Turn up the heat to medium and toss the spaghetti around until all the water is absorbed and the pasta is cooked al dente. Add more pasta water if needed.

7   Serve topped with more parsley and pangrattato, if using. Add a sprinkle of Maldon salt.

CACIO E PEPE

SERVES 2 TO 4

Cacio e pepe is probably the most popular pasta dish in Rome. On countless occasions when I lived in Rome, I felt my mouth watering wildly, watching people eat it up while knowing that I couldn't have any, as *cacio e pepe* means "cheese and pepper."

Of course, my version has no dairy cream or cheese. It's just a clean vegan cheese sauce with lots of black pepper—and it's the second-most popular dish on the Pura Vita menu.

1 cup raw, unsalted cashews

½ cup filtered water

¼ cup lemon juice

1 tablespoon apple cider vinegar

2 teaspoons nutritional yeast

2 teaspoons minced garlic

1 teaspoon sea salt, plus 2 tablespoons for the pasta water

1½ teaspoons black pepper, plus more for topping

¼ cup extra-virgin olive oil

1 pound bucatini

Chopped fresh parsley

1   Soak the cashews in water for a minimum of 4 hours. Drain and rinse well before using.

2   In a large pot, bring 4 to 6 quarts of water to a rolling boil.

3   Meanwhile, in a high-speed blender, combine the cashews, water, lemon juice, vinegar, yeast, garlic, 2 teaspoons of the salt, and the pepper. Blend until smooth.

4   With the blender running on low speed, slowly add the olive oil until smooth.

5   Add the remaining 2 tablespoons of salt to the boiling water. Add the bucatini and cook until very al dente, a little more than half the recommended cooking time.

6   Pour all the cacio e pepe sauce into a large sauté pan and warm it over low heat for 3 to 4 minutes, just enough to make it piping hot.

7   Use pasta tongs to transfer the bucatini to the sauté pan and add ½ cup of the pasta cooking water.

8   Cook the bucatini in the sauce, tossing it around until it absorbs all the water and is perfectly al dente. Check to make sure the pasta does not overcook. Add more pasta water if needed.

9   Top with parsley and pepper.

SPAGHETTI
alla PUTTANESCA

SERVES 2 TO 4

A funny tidbit about puttanesca: in Italian it roughly translates to "the style of a whore." The name comes from the Italian word *puttana,* which means "prostitute," and *puttanesca* is basically derived from that. It's said that the dish may have been invented in one of the bordellos in Naples, basically just to make a quick meal to be eaten between servicing clients, if you know what I'm saying.

---

1 In a large pot, bring 4 to 6 quarts of water to a rolling boil.

2 Meanwhile, in a large sauté pan heat the olive oil over medium-low heat. Sauté the garlic, cherry tomatoes, olives, capers, parsley, pinch of salt, pepper, and red pepper flakes. Continue to cook for 4 to 5 minutes.

3 Add the marinara sauce and continue to cook.

4 Add the remaining 2 tablespoons of salt to the boiling water. Add the spaghetti and cook until very al dente, a little more than half the recommended cooking time.

5 Use pasta tongs to transfer the spaghetti to the sauté pan and add ½ cup of the pasta cooking water.

6 Continue to cook the spaghetti in the sauce, tossing around the pasta until it absorbs all the water and the pasta is perfectly al dente. Check to make sure the spaghetti does not overcook. Add more pasta water if needed. The sauce should stay juicy!

7 Serve topped with parsley.

2 tablespoons extra-virgin olive oil

1 teaspoon minced garlic

1 cup halved cherry tomatoes

½ cup small, pitted Gaeta or Kalamata olives

2 tablespoons capers, drained if in brine, rinsed if salt packed

1 tablespoon chopped fresh parsley, plus more for topping

Pinch of sea salt, plus 2 tablespoons for the pasta water

Pinch of black pepper

1 teaspoon red pepper flakes

2 cups Marinara Sauce (page 37)

1 pound spaghetti

WHEN IN ROME

When I was seventeen years old, I embarked on one of the most epic trips of my life. My father had to travel to Europe for business and he decided to bring me along as an assistant. The company he was working for held a large convention every year, and my father's job was to choose where they would go, where they would stay, where they would eat, and so on. That involved a lot of research, and so the trip took quite a long time!

One of our stops was Paris, which, at the time, was not very vegan friendly. I almost starved to death. No matter how much I begged waiters for any type of food without dairy, the answer was always just non—ce n'est pas possible! They wouldn't even make me a potato without soaking it in butter. It was so frustrating because although the city was beautiful, I was always so hungry. I lost seven pounds in five days.

Our next stop was Rome—and my first order of business was food. On day one we went to a restaurant in the area called Trastevere (still one of my favorite areas of Rome). I said to the waiter, "Please, I am very hungry. I can't have any meat and I can't have any dairy, and I can't have any eggs or butter. . ."

The waiter just put his hand up with a little Italian gesture and said, "I understand what you don't want, but what do you want?"

"I just want some pasta and maybe some vegetables, whatever, anything that you can make that doesn't contain those other ingredients," I replied.

The waiter said, "No problem," and for the next three hours food proceeded to come out from the kitchen nonstop, a feast beyond feasts, as if I were the queen of the city. There was every vegetable dish I could think of: zucchini and peppers and eggplant and chicory and beautiful, fresh, amazing dishes that were clearly made with just beautiful olive oil and a little bit of garlic. All wonderful, all super simple, all vegan.

On top of all that was a huge plate of penne arrabbiata, which to this day is one of my favorite pasta dishes.

PENNE ALL'ARRABBIATA

SERVES 2 TO 4

Arrabbiata actually means "angry" in Italian, but that's just a way of letting you know that it's a spicy dish.

1 In a large pot, bring 4 to 6 quarts of water to a rolling boil.

2 Meanwhile, in a large sauté pan over medium-low heat, heat the olive oil. Sauté the garlic, arrabbiata paste (depending on preferred spice level), cherry tomatoes, the pinch of salt, and pepper for 4 to 5 minutes.

3 Add the marinara sauce and continue to sauté.

4 Add the remaining 2 tablespoons of salt to the boiling water. Add the penne and cook until very al dente, a little more than half the recommended cooking time.

5 Use pasta tongs to transfer the penne to the sauté pan and add ½ cup of the pasta cooking water.

6 Continue to cook the penne in the sauce, tossing around the pasta until it absorbs all the water and is perfectly al dente. Check to make sure the penne does not overcook. Add more pasta water if needed.

7 Serve topped with parsley.

ARRABBIATA PASTE

Mix the chili paste, smoked paprika, red pepper flakes, and olive oil together in a bowl. Let sit for 1 hour.

TIP: Make extra so you always have this on hand, and you can make any dish smoky and spicy in an instant! You can store arrabbiata paste in the refrigerator for up to 6 months.

2 tablespoons extra-virgin olive oil

1 teaspoon minced garlic

2 to 3 teaspoons Arrabbiata Paste (recipe follows)

1 cup halved cherry tomatoes

Pinch of sea salt, plus 2 tablespoons for the pasta water

Pinch of black pepper

2 cups Marinara Sauce (page 37)

1 pound penne

Chopped fresh parsley

ARRABBIATA PASTE

½ cup Calabrian chili paste

2 tablespoons smoked paprika

1½ tablespoons crushed red pepper flakes

¼ cup extra-virgin olive oil

PESTO CAVATELLI

SERVES 2 TO 4

This is one of my mother's all-time favorite pasta dishes, and she made it regularly while I was growing up. Of course, this pesto recipe can go on top of any pasta shape. Pick your favorite and toss it in your homemade pesto sauce.

2 tablespoons extra-virgin olive oil

1 teaspoon minced garlic

1 cup halved cherry tomatoes (optional)

Pinch of sea salt, plus 2 tablespoons for the pasta water

Pinch of black pepper

2 cups Classic Pesto (page 38)

1 pound cavatelli

Macadamia Parmigiano for garnish (page 35)

1   In a large pot, bring 4 to 6 quarts of water to a rolling boil.

2   Meanwhile, in a large sauté pan over medium-low heat, heat the olive oil. Sauté the garlic, cherry tomatoes, if using, the pinch of salt, and pepper for 4 to 5 minutes.

3   Add the pesto sauce and continue to sauté over medium-low heat.

4   Add the remaining 2 tablespoons of salt to the boiling water. Add the cavatelli and cook until very al dente, a little more than half the recommended cooking time.

5   Use a slotted spoon to transfer the cavatelli to the sauté pan and add ½ cup of the pasta cooking water.

6   Continue to cook the cavatelli in the sauce, tossing around the pasta until it absorbs all the water and is perfectly al dente. Check to make sure the cavatelli does not overcook. Add more pasta water if needed.

7   Garnish with macadamia parmigiano.

PESTO CALABRESE

with BUCATINI

SERVES 2 TO 4

Everything about this dish of pasta makes me happy. It's nostalgic because of my grandma. It's comforting because that's what bucatini does for me—it is so savory, silky, spicy, and satiating. The dish is traditionally vegetarian, using ricotta cheese. But of course I have to take it a step further and ensure no animals are involved. Use my Almond Ricotta (page 33) and you will not miss a beat.

2 tablespoons extra-virgin olive oil

1 teaspoon minced garlic

Pinch of sea salt, plus 2 tablespoons for the pasta water

Pinch of black pepper

1½ cups Pesto Calabrese sauce (page 39)

1 pound bucatini

Fresh basil or microbasil for topping

1   In a large pot, bring 4 to 6 quarts of water to a rolling boil.

2   Meanwhile, in a large sauté pan over medium-low heat, heat the olive oil. Sauté the garlic, pinch of salt, and pepper for 4 to 5 minutes.

3   Add the pesto calabrese sauce and continue to sauté over medium-low heat.

4   Add the remaining 2 tablespoons of salt to the boiling water. Add the bucatini and cook until very al dente, a little more than half the recommended cooking time.

5   Use pasta tongs to transfer the bucatini to the sauté pan and add 1 cup of the pasta cooking water.

6   Cook the bucatini in the sauce, tossing around the pasta until it absorbs all the water and is perfectly al dente. Check to make sure the pasta does not overcook. Add more pasta water if needed.

7   Serve topped with basil.

FETTUCCINE ALFREDO

SERVES 2 TO 4

Fettuccine Alfredo, contrary to popular belief, was created in Rome, Italy. Although Italians argue that this dish is not a true Italian pasta dish, and you'll seldom find it in Italy, it actually is. Regardless, this dish certainly stole the attention of Americans: We took it and ran! Alfredo's creamy texture and simplicity make it so easy to fall in love with it. Here is a perfect example of using cashews to make cream. Cashews are fatty but so light in flavor that they easily turn into a simple, silky cream sauce.

Alfredo Sauce (page 44) also makes for an excellent baked pasta dish. You can find the recipe for my Baked Ziti Alfredo on page 190.

4 tablespoons vegan butter

1 tablespoon minced garlic

Pinch of sea salt, plus 2 tablespoons for the pasta water

Pinch of black pepper

1½ cups Alfredo Sauce (page 44)

1 pound fettuccine

Chopped fresh parsley, for topping

Macadamia Parmigiano (page 35), for topping

1   In a large pot, bring 4 to 6 quarts of water to a rolling boil.

2   Meanwhile, heat the vegan butter in a large sauté pan over medium-low heat. Sauté the garlic, pinch of salt, and pepper for 3 to 4 minutes.

3   Add the Alfredo sauce and continue to sauté over medium-low heat.

4   Add the remaining 2 tablespoons of salt to the boiling water. Add the fettuccine and cook until very al dente, a little more than half the recommended cooking time.

5   Use pasta tongs to transfer the fettuccine to the sauté pan and add 1 cup of the pasta cooking water. Cook the pasta in the sauce, tossing around the pasta until it absorbs all the water and is perfectly al dente. Check to make sure the fettuccine does not overcook. Add more pasta water if needed.

6   Serve topped with freshly chopped parsley and a sprinkle of macadamia parmigiano.

Left to right: Cousin Carmelino, Daddy, Uncle Tony, me, Zio Renzo, and Eduardo, in Trastevere, Rome, celebrating my twenty-seventh birthday. Photo by Mom.

SEARCHING FOR A JOB IN ROME

I moved to Rome in April 2005. As much as I love the food of New York, the food in Rome and the surrounding cities is truly something special. Its uniqueness derives in part from the way Italians grow their vegetables, the way they prepare their food, the way they keep everything organic and natural whenever possible. Everything just tastes so wonderful.

One of my favorite parts of Rome was the farmers markets. Tomatoes basking in the sunlight made me understand that a tomato is indeed a fruit and not a vegetable; they are so sweet and juicy, and the texture is completely different.

Or course I immediately tracked down all the vegetarian and vegan restaurants—which meant about five—to see if I could get a job, any job at all, in the kitchen. I wanted to observe, experience, and learn as much as I could. I didn't even care if I made money at that point. But one after the other, they turned me down.

After my final rejection I went outside and noticed a man dressed in chef whites, so I knew he was from the kitchen. He was smoking a cigarette and actually spoke English. He asked me kindly what I was trying to do. I explained that I just wanted to have the experience of observing a kitchen in Rome to understand how it's different from one in America, and to learn as much as I could. Ah, he said, that's nice, but I would never get hired in a kitchen in Italy.

"We don't hire women to work in a professional kitchen," he added. "Only men can work in a professional kitchen."

I couldn't believe it. His tone was so matter-of-fact. But then I realized, thank God he said that, because I'd actually been thinking that there was something wrong with me. It turns out all that was wrong with me was that I was female.

Now, this was twenty years ago, and things have changed. But it changed me, too, as I decided that there was nothing in the world that was more motivating than somebody telling me that I couldn't do something. In a way, I owe that man a lot.

LEMON PEPPER CREAM PACCHERI

with SPRING PEAS AND PISTACHIO

SERVES 2 TO 4

This dish is heavily influenced by the cuisine of Sicily, where you will find a wealth of flavors, from the "green gold" of Bronte pistachios to the fragrant citrus delights of lemons and oranges. The gorgeous local herbs intoxicate your senses as you walk through Sicily's markets. It is a place that should immediately move up to the top of your travel list.

This dish was created after a walk through the Ballarò market in Palermo. The smell of this pasta dish will likely seduce your dinner partner, so be careful and choose wisely!

LEMON PEPPER SAUCE

1   Soak the cashews in water for a minimum of 4 hours. Drain and rinse well before using.

2   In a high-speed blender, combine the cashews, water, lemon juice, vinegar, yeast, mint, basil, garlic, salt, pepper, chili flakes, and lemon zest. Blend until smooth.

3   With the blender running on low speed, slowly add the olive oil until smooth.

FOR THE PASTA

1   In a large pot, bring 4 to 6 quarts of water to a rolling boil.

2   Meanwhile, heat the olive oil in a large sauté pan over medium-low heat. Sauté the peas with the pinch of salt and pepper for 2 to 3 minutes, just until hot.

Continued

LEMON PEPPER SAUCE

1 cup raw, unsalted cashews

½ cup filtered water

½ cup lemon juice

1 tablespoon apple cider vinegar

2 teaspoons nutritional yeast

3 tablespoons packed mint leaves

3 tablespoons packed basil leaves

2 teaspoons minced garlic

2 teaspoons sea salt

2 teaspoons black pepper

⅛ teaspoon chili flakes

2 teaspoons lemon zest

¼ cup extra virgin olive oil

FOR THE PASTA

2 tablespoons extra-virgin olive oil

Pinch of sea salt, plus 2 tablespoons for the pasta water

Pinch of black pepper

½ cup spring peas (blanched fresh, or frozen)

1½ cup Lemon Pepper Sauce (recipe above)

1 cup pasta water

1 pound paccheri

Pangrattato (page 51) for topping

Roasted Pistachio Crumble (page 42) for topping

Fresh mint, chopped or torn, for topping

3   Add 1½ cups of the lemon pepper sauce and continue to cook over medium-low heat.

4   Add the remaining 2 tablespoons of salt to the boiling water. Add the paccheri and cook until very al dente, a little more than half the recommended cooking time.

5   Use pasta tongs to transfer the pasta to the sauté pan and add 1 cup of the pasta cooking water.

6   Continue to cook the paccheri in the sauce, tossing around the pasta until it absorbs all the water and is perfectly al dente. Check to make sure the paccheri does not overcook. Add more pasta water if needed.

7   Serve topped with pangrattato, pistachio crumble, and mint.

TAGLIATELLE
in BUTTERNUT CREAM SAUCE

SERVES 2 TO 4

Seasonality is very important in my kitchen. I pay attention to what's being offered at the local farmers markets so I can ensure every dish uses the freshest version of the vegetables. During fall or winter, squash always becomes a focus. So, to make a great cream sauce, I turned to butternut squash. Like most of my other sauces, it's cashew-based and surprisingly easy to make: All you need is a really strong blender or food processor.

I like to use this sauce on a ribbonlike pasta, such as tagliatelle or fettuccine. It's a wonderful way to sneak some vegetables into your kids' meals, because they probably won't realize that the sauce is made from squash.

There are several components to this dish and all can be made ahead of time.

BUTTERNUT SQUASH CREAM SAUCE

1   Soak the cashews in water for a minimum of 4 hours. Drain and rinse well before using.

2   Preheat the oven to 375°F.

3   Place the diced squash on a baking sheet.

4   Mix together the vegan butter, garlic, and 1 teaspoon each of salt and pepper in a bowl. Spread it over the squash.

5   Bake until the squash is fully cooked (fork tender), 25 to 30 minutes. Allow to cool.

6   Place the soaked cashews, water, lemon juice, yeast, garlic, and remaining 2 teaspoons each of salt and pepper in a high-speed blender and blend on medium-high until smooth.

7   With the machine running on low, pour in the ¼ cup melted vegan butter to emulsify.

8   Add the cooked and cooled squash and blend until smooth.

Continued

BUTTERNUT SQUASH CREAM SAUCE

1 cup raw, unsalted cashews

3 cups butternut squash cut into ½-inch dice

2 tablespoons vegan butter, melted, plus ¼ cup

2 teaspoons minced garlic

3 teaspoons sea salt

1 teaspoon black pepper

½ cup filtered water

¼ cup lemon juice

1 tablespoon nutritional yeast

1 tablespoon minced garlic

NOTE: If you prefer, you can also use kabocha squash, which is also very creamy and delicious, and slightly less sweet.

CRISPY SAGE

1   Preheat the oven to 375°F, if it isn't already at this temperature.

2   Toss the sage leaves with the olive oil and salt.

3   Spread the sage on a baking sheet and bake for 3 to 5 minutes, or until crispy.

TAGLIATELLE

1   In a large pot, bring 4 to 6 quarts of water to a rolling boil.

2   Meanwhile, melt the vegan butter in a large sauté pan over medium-low heat. Sauté the garlic and kale with the pinch of salt and the pepper for 4 to 5 minutes.

3   Add 2 cups of butternut cream sauce and continue to sauté over medium-low heat.

4   Add the remaining 2 tablespoons of salt to the boiling water. Add the tagliatelle and cook until very al dente, a little more than half the recommended cooking time.

5   Use pasta tongs to transfer the tagliatelle to the sauté pan and add ½ cup of the pasta cooking water.

6   Cook the pasta in the sauce, tossing around the tagliatelle until it absorbs all the water and is perfectly al dente. Check to make sure the pasta does not overcook. Add more pasta water if needed.

7   Serve topped with crispy sage and spiced pepitas.

CRISPY SAGE

1 cup loose, fresh sage leaves

1 tablespoon extra-virgin olive oil

Pinch of sea salt

TAGLIATELLE

¼ cup vegan butter

2 teaspoons minced garlic

Pinch of sea salt, plus 2 tablespoons for the pasta water

Pinch of black pepper

2 cups kale, cut into thin strips

2 cups Butternut Squash Cream Sauce (see previous page)

1 pound Fresh Tagliatelle (page 141)

Crispy sage (see above), for topping

Spiced Pepitas (page 57), for topping

LINGUINE DI MARE
in GARLIC WHITE WINE SAUCE

SERVES 2 TO 4

I don't know why I loved this dish so much when I was young, because I actually never ate the clams. I would pick out those little rubbery pieces and place them on the side, and that was before I even became vegan.

I think it was the wonderfully ocean-air-salty and light linguine that really hooked me. Even after I stopped eating animals, this dish always remained in the back of my mind.

Several years ago, just before the restaurant opened, I decided to give it a whirl. I used king oyster mushrooms, which have a very light, sea-like taste, but are neither fishy nor mushroomy, and a garlic and white wine sauce. Ta-da! It tasted more like my mother's linguine with clam sauce than any replica I've ever tried; and, on top of that, it's one of the top-selling dishes at my restaurant!

KING OYSTER MUSHROOM STEM SCALLOPS

1. Remove the mushroom stems. Set the caps aside. Cut the mushroom stems crosswise into ¾-inch-thick slices and put them in a bowl.

2. Marinate them in the olive oil, garlic, lemon juice, paprika, salt, and pepper in the refrigerator for 4 hours or more.

3. Preheat the oven to 350°F.

4. Spread the stems slices on a baking sheet and roast for 15 to 20 minutes.

5. Chop the mushroom caps into tiny pieces. These will represent the "clams" in the finished pasta! Cover and refrigerate the diced caps until you are ready to make the pasta.

Continued

KING OYSTER MUSHROOM STEM SCALLOPS

1 pound king oyster mushrooms

2 tablespoons extra-virgin olive oil

1 tablespoon minced garlic

1½ teaspoons lemon juice

2 teaspoons smoked paprika

2 teaspoons sea salt

½ teaspoon black pepper

LINGUINE IN GARLIC WHITE WINE SAUCE

¼ cup extra virgin olive oil

2 tablespoons vegan butter

1 cup thinly sliced (into half-moons) shallots

2 tablespoons minced garlic

1 tablespoon fresh thyme leaves

1 teaspoon sea salt

½ teaspoon dulse

½ teaspoon red chili flakes (optional)

1 cup dry white wine

1½ cups king oyster mushroom caps

1 pound linguine

Pangrattato (page 51) to taste

¼ cup chopped fresh parsley

LINGUINE IN GARLIC WHITE WINE SAUCE

1 In a large pot, bring 4 to 6 quarts of water to a rolling boil.

2 Meanwhile, heat the vegan butter and olive oil in a large sauté pan over medium-low heat. Sauté the shallots, garlic, thyme, 2 teaspoons of the salt, the pepper, dulse, and chili flakes, if using, for 7 to 8 minutes.

3 Add the wine to the pan and cook for another 8 to 10 minutes to allow all the alcohol to burn off.

4 Add the chopped mushroom caps and continue to sauté over medium-low heat.

5 Add the remaining 2 tablespoons of salt to the boiling water. Add the linguine and cook until very al dente, a little more than half the recommended cooking time.

6 Use pasta tongs to transfer the pasta to the sauté pan and add 1 cup of the pasta cooking water. Cook the linguine in the sauce, tossing around the linguine until it absorbs all the water and is perfectly al dente.

7 Meanwhile, make sure your mushroom stem scallops are still hot. If necessary, you can reheat them in a 400°F oven or grill for a few minutes on each side.

8 Spoon the mushroom scallops over the linguine.

9 Top with pangrattato and lots of parsley.

PENNE *alla* VODKA

SERVES 2 TO 4

When I was a really young pre-vegan girl, I had this notion that it was cool to drink alcohol for some reason. Maybe it was because the adults always had wine with dinner—I was even allowed a tiny little glass of red wine myself. If we went out to an Italian restaurant and the option was penne alla vodka, I always ordered it because alcohol was part of the sauce, and that made me feel grown-up. At the time I had no idea how cooking worked and didn't realize that the alcohol in the vodka is burned off while the pasta is being cooked. Still, it made me feel cool, and that was what mattered.

2 tablespoons extra-virgin olive oil

½ cup finely diced yellow onion

1 tablespoon minced garlic

Pinch of red chili flakes

3½ cups D.O.P. San Marzano tomatoes, slightly broken up

6 tablespoons vodka

½ cup Cashew Cream (page 56)

¼ cup chopped fresh basil

2 teaspoons sea salt, plus 2 tablespoons for the pasta water

¼ teaspoon black pepper

1 pound penne

Chili Oil (page 52, optional)

1   In large pot, bring 4 to 6 quarts of water to a rolling boil.

2   Meanwhile, in a large sauté pan, heat the olive oil over medium heat. Sauté the onion, garlic, and red chili flakes for 10 minutes, or until the onion is translucent.

3   Add the tomatoes and vodka and simmer for 1 hour over low heat.

4   Add the cashew cream and bring to a simmer.

5   Add the basil, 2 teaspoons of the salt, and the pepper. Taste for salt.

6   Add the remaining 2 tablespoons of salt to the boiling water. Add the penne and cook until very al dente, a little more than half the recommended cooking time.

7   Use pasta tongs to transfer the penne to the sauté pan and add ½ cup of the pasta cooking water. Cook the pasta in the sauce, tossing around the pasta until it absorbs all the water and is perfectly al dente, checking to make sure the penne does not overcook. Add more pasta water if needed.

8   Serve topped with a heavy drizzle of homemade chili oil if you like it hot!

LOVE, ITALIAN STYLE

When I was seventeen, while traveling in Italy with my father, we decided to extend his business trip and see some relatives. At that point I had been with my father every second of every day, day in and day out, so when we arrived at Rome's Piazza Navona, my father said, "I have an idea. Why don't you walk that way and I'll walk this way and we'll meet on the other side." I said, "Great!"

We took about five steps in opposite directions. On the sixth step, I met a very handsome boy. I could tell by the way he was dressed (all in black) that we were probably into the same type of music and other such things. But when he started talking to me, I also realized he didn't speak a word of English, and I didn't speak any Italian. Somehow we made it work. We kept attempting to communicate, giggling all the while because we were just trying to say things without using words.

We walked around the Piazza Navona for what seemed like forever, just lapping around and around and passing my father, whose rolling eyes suggested he was saying, "Geez, what did I do?" The boy and I exchanged information, and after that trip he wrote the most beautiful letter I've ever received in my life, in the most Italian way possible, something an American boy would never dream of doing because it just wouldn't be cool. I could tell he had written the whole thing in Italian and then translated it word for word (probably using a dictionary) into English. It didn't make for poetry, but still, I melted into a puddle. I was in love. He proceeded to write me letters like this one a couple times a month.

About a year later, when I was in my first year at the School of Visual Arts, I sold my first photograph for a thousand dollars, so I immediately flew back to Italy because I wanted to see my boy. It was an incredible experience. We spent three straight weeks together in his hometown just outside Naples. The food that boy made for me was amazing—he learned everything he knew from his mother and his grandmother, just as every Italian boy would tell you.

One of his best meals he cooked up was pasta e ceci, which is pasta and chickpeas. It's a very simple dish that my grandmother also made when I was young, but I never knew the recipe. But this was one of the most delicious things ever, just pasta, chickpeas, a little fresh rosemary, and some sun-dried tomatoes. Pasta e ceci. It will always remind me of my Italian boy. (Although the story took a different turn once the boy learned English many years later and we ended up in New York together. Once I understood what he was actually saying, I decided to send him back to Italy.)

PASTA E CECI

SERVES 2 TO 4

Pasta e ceci is classic southern Italian comfort food at its best. In Italy, this category of food is known as *cucina povera* ("poor kitchen"), or peasant food. These types of dishes are designed to be inexpensive while fully nourishing and deeply satisfying.

1   In a large sauté pan, heat the olive oil over medium-low heat. Sauté the garlic, onion, tomato, rosemary, chili flakes, chickpeas, vinegar, sea salt, and pepper over medium-low heat for 10 minutes.

2   After 10 minutes, crush some of the chickpeas with a fork. Crush as many as you would like, depending on how thick versus textured you desire your dish to be.

3   Add the water to the pan. Increase the heat and bring to a boil.

4   Add the ditalini to the pan. Cook the pasta in the sauce, tossing it around until the ditalini is perfectly al dente, checking to make sure the pasta does not overcook and adding more water if needed. Stir constantly to ensure the pasta does not stick to the bottom.

5   Add the baby spinach and parsley and cook until the greens are wilted, 3 to 4 minutes.

6   Top with a heavy drizzle of olive oil, some macadamia parmigiano, parsley, and Maldon salt.

TIP: If you don't have ditalini or other small pasta, you can break spaghetti into small pieces for this dish—it works perfectly!

½ cup extra-virgin olive oil, plus more for topping

2 tablespoons minced garlic

1 cup finely diced yellow onion

¼ cup finely chopped sun-dried tomato, in olive oil

1 tablespoon fresh rosemary leaves

1 teaspoon red chili flakes

Two 15.5-ounce cans chickpeas, drained

2 teaspoons apple cider vinegar

1 tablespoon sea salt

1 teaspoon black pepper

4 cups filtered water

1 pound ditalini pasta (or pastina or orzo)

2 cups chopped baby spinach (or kale or chard)

½ cup of chopped fresh parsley, plus extra for topping

Macadamia Parmigiano (page 35), for topping

Maldon salt, for topping

FUSILLI PRIMAVERA

SERVES 2 TO 4

Primavera means "spring" in Italian, but this dish is perfect any time of the year. I have specific vegetables listed here, but you can mix and match with any of your seasonal favorites.

1 In a large pot, bring 4 to 6 quarts of water to a rolling boil.

2 Meanwhile, heat the olive oil in a large sauté pan over medium heat. Sauté the shallot, garlic, thyme, 2 teaspoons of salt, pepper, and chili flakes for 5 to 8 minutes.

3 Add the vegan butter, broth, and lemon juice and cook for another 5 to 6 minutes.

4 Add the wine and cook for 5 minutes, or until all the alcohol burns off.

5 Add broccoli florets, red bell peppers, spring peas, cherry tomatoes, parsley, and chopped basil to the sauté pan and mix well. Cook for another 4 to 5 minutes.

6 Add the remaining 2 tablespoons of salt to the boiling water. Add the fusilli and cook until very al dente, a little more than half the recommended cooking time.

7 Use pasta tongs to transfer the fusilli to the sauté pan and add ½ cup of the pasta cooking water. Cook the pasta in the sauce, tossing around the fusilli until it absorbs all the water and is perfectly al dente. Add more pasta water if needed. Check to make sure the pasta does not overcook. Taste for salt.

8 Top with macadamia parmigiano and basil.

¼ cup extra-virgin olive oil

1 cup finely diced shallot

¼ cup minced garlic

1 tablespoon fresh thyme leaves

2 teaspoons sea salt, plus 2 tablespoons for the pasta water

2 teaspoons black pepper

1 teaspoon red chili flakes

¼ cup vegan butter

½ cup vegetable broth (I like Imagine No-Chicken)

¼ cup lemon juice

½ cup dry white wine

½ cup blanched broccoli florets

½ cup diced red bell pepper

½ cup spring peas

1 cup halved cherry tomatoes

¼ cup chopped fresh parsley

¼ cup chopped fresh basil

1 pound fusilli

Macadamia Parmigiano (page 35)

Torn fresh basil for garnish

TAGLIATELLE *alla* BOLOGNESE

SERVES 2 TO 4

Bolognese is a typical classic Italian pasta sauce normally made with ground beef or pork, slowly cooked with a mix of onion, carrots, celery, tomatoes, spices, and herbs. For the vegan version, you can use premade fake meat products, but I prefer whole foods that are grown from the ground. So for my bolognese I use lentils and walnuts to create that perfect meaty texture.

The lentils should be cooked to their desired softness before you make the sauce. I tend to use green lentils, but you can also try other types of lentils, such as black ones. (You don't want to use red lentils because they're too soft and squishy.)

The fresh herbs should be added right after you take the sauce off the stove.

For the most part, I prefer bolognese sauce with fresh tagliatelle (page 141). You can also use any other ribbonlike pasta, such as fettuccine or pappardelle.

___

1 In a large pot, bring 4 to 6 quarts of water to a rolling boil.

2 Meanwhile, heat the olive oil in a large sauté pan over medium heat. Sauté the onion, celery, carrot, garlic, 1 teaspoon of the salt, smoked paprika, oregano, pepper, thyme, and nutritional yeast for 10 minutes.

3 Add the wine and sauté for 5 minutes to allow the alcohol to burn off.

2 tablespoons extra-virgin olive oil

½ cup finely diced yellow onion

¼ cup finely diced celery

¼ cup finely diced carrot

2 teaspoons minced garlic

1 teaspoon sea salt, plus 2 tablespoons for the pasta water

½ teaspoon smoked paprika

½ teaspoon dried oregano

½ teaspoon black pepper

1 tsp chopped fresh thyme

1 teaspoon nutritional yeast

2 tablespoons dry red wine

½ cup walnut pieces

½ cup cooked green lentils

1¼ cups Marinara Sauce (page 37)

¼ cup chopped fresh basil

¼ cup chopped fresh parsley

1 pound Fresh Tagliatelle (page 141), or any other ribbonlike pasta

Macadamia Parmigiano (page 35, optional)

NOTE: Either pulse your walnuts in a food processor until they are in small pieces (not a paste) or put them in a ziplock bag and smash them with a hammer. (Be careful not to hurt yourself!)

4   Add the walnut pieces and lentils and sauté for another 5 minutes.

5   Add the marinara sauce. Bring to a boil. Reduce the heat and simmer for 10 minutes.

6   Add the basil and parsley. Taste for salt.

7   Add the remaining 2 tablespoons of salt to the boiling water. Add the tagliatelle and cook until very al dente, a little more than half the recommended cooking time.

8   Use pasta tongs to transfer the tagliatelle to the sauté pan and add 1 cup of the pasta cooking water. Cook the pasta in the sauce, tossing around the tagliatelle until it absorbs all the water and is perfectly al dente. Check to make sure the pasta does not overcook. Add more pasta water if needed.

9   Top with macadamia parmigiano, if using.

BAKED ZITI

Try going to southern Italy and not running into baked ziti. It's everywhere. And the same was true at my family's house: everyone made it, with just slight variations, for every party we ever had since the beginning of time. That's because it truly is a great dish to serve at any large gathering. You can prepare it in advance, it's so simple to make, and I've never met anyone who didn't love it.

Baked ziti, or *ziti al forno,* has a long history. From as early as the late Middle Ages, ziti al forno was served at the banquets and palaces of nobles for ceremonies and celebrations. Now it is our responsibility to carry on this tradition and serve it to our family and friends at our own celebrations.

I am providing two different versions of this famous baked pasta dish, but don't let that stop you from experimenting and creating your own. You can try this dish with vodka sauce, add other vegetables or mushrooms to the mix, or even give it a twist by adding a plant-based sausage or alternative meat crumble! My favorite store-bought plant-based meat products are Abbot's. They have the cleanest list of ingredients for these types of products and I appreciate that. If you can find their ground "beef," try adding it into the baked ziti and watch the magic happen.

Whatever you decide, do not feel intimidated. Baked ziti is easy to make and difficult to mess up. As always, it's all about the sauce.

BAKED ZITI "TRADITIONAL"

SERVES 12

1. In a large pot, bring 4 to 6 quarts of water to a rolling boil. Add the salt.

2. Add the ziti and cook until al dente. Drain and rinse the pasta under cool water to stop the cooking process.

3. Preheat the oven to 375°F.

4. In a large mixing bowl, combine the cooked ziti, marinara sauce, cashew ricotta, and 3 cups of the cashew mozzarella. Use a large wooden spoon to gently mix the cooked ziti with the sauce and cheeses until all the ingredients are evenly combined.

5. Transfer the pasta mixture into a 9 by 13-inch baking pan.

6. Top the pasta with the remaining 2 cups of cashew mozzarella, spreading it evenly across the top of the pasta. You can add more cheese or sauce to taste if necessary.

7. Cover the pan with a lid or foil and bake for 25 to 30 minutes. Remove the cover and bake for another 5 to 10 minutes, until the cashew mozzarella is lightly browned on top.

8. Serve with extra marinara sauce.

¼ cup sea salt

2 pounds ziti

4 cups Marinara Sauce (page 37), plus extra for serving

6 cups Cashew Ricotta (page 33)

5 cups Cashew Mozzarella (page 34)

BAKED ZITI ALFREDO

SERVES 12

1 In a large pot, bring 4 to 6 quarts of water to a rolling boil.

2 Add the salt, then add the ziti and cook until al dente.

3 Drain and rinse the pasta under cool water to stop the cooking process. Set aside.

4 Preheat the oven to 375°F.

5 In a large mixing bowl, combine the ziti, Alfredo sauce, cashew ricotta, 3 cups of the cashew mozzarella, and the asparagus. Using a large wooden spoon, gently mix the cooked ziti with the sauce and cheeses until all the ingredients are evenly combined. Transfer the pasta into a 9 by 13-inch baking pan.

6 Top the pasta with the remaining 2 cups of cashew mozzarella, spreading it evenly across the top of the pasta. You can add more sauce or cheese to taste if necessary.

7 Top with pangrattato, sprinkling it evenly across the pan.

8 Cover the pan with a lid or foil and bake for 25 to 30 minutes. Remove the cover and bake for another 5 to 10 minutes, until the mozzarella and pangrattato reach a light golden brown.

¼ cup sea salt

2 pounds ziti

4 cups Alfredo Sauce (page 44)

6 cups Cashew Ricotta (page 33)

5 cups Cashew Mozzarella (page 34)

4 cups Roasted Lemon Asparagus (page 115), cut into ½-inch pieces (or other seasonal vegetable)

3 cups Pangrattato (page 51)

I
SECONDI

Eggplant Parmigiana, *Page 194*

EGGPLANT PARMIGIANA

Eggplant parmigiana was my grandpa's specialty. Even people who don't like eggplant always find this delicious.

Grandpa always made it in one of two different ways. One was the traditional Neapolitan way, which meant layering it in a pan like a lasagna—very cheese heavy, incredibly delicious, and naturally gluten-free. This is my favorite version and the one I will explain first!

The second version of Grandpa's recipes for eggplant parm means breading and pan-frying it, which is equally scrumptious. Honestly, I can't decide which way I like it better, so I'm sharing this version of the recipe with you as well. Hopefully you can experience a little bit of my grandpa's love of eggplant through his tried-and-true traditions.

PARMIGIANA *di* MELANZANE
THE TRADITIONAL NEAPOLITAN WAY
(GLUTEN FREE)

SERVES 9 TO 12

1. Peel the eggplant and cut it lengthwise—top to bottom—into ¼- to ½-inch slices.

2. Sprinkle the salt evenly over the eggplant and let it rest for 30 minutes. After 30 minutes, the eggplant should be covered in water. Wash the eggplant completely and gently pat dry.

3. Preheat the oven to 350°F.

4. Add the flour to a medium mixing bowl and dredge the eggplant slices in it.

5. Brush the olive oil on a large cookie sheet or sheet pan. If all the eggplant doesn't fit, use two pans.

6. Bake the eggplant in the prepared pan for 12 minutes. Cool.

7. In a 9 by 13-inch baking pan, layer the ingredients in the following order:

8. Spread 1 cup of marinara sauce in the pan. Add one layer of eggplant slices, overlapping the edges to completely cover the sauce. Spread 2 cups of cashew ricotta over the eggplant, then spread 1 cup cashew mozzarella over the ricotta. Sprinkle with ¼ cup macadamia parmigiano. Top with 8 basil leaves.

9. Add another layer of eggplant slices. Spread another cup of marinara sauce evenly over the eggplant. Spread another 2 cups of cashew ricotta on the marinara sauce, followed by 1 cup of cashew mozzarella. Sprinkle with ¼ cup of macadamia parmigiano. Top with another 8 basil leaves.

10. Add a final layer of eggplant slices, 1 cup of marinara sauce, and 2 cups of cashew mozzarella.

11. Increase the oven temperature to 375°F.

12. Cover the eggplant with a lid or foil and bake for 45 minutes. Remove the cover and bake for another 10 minutes. Let it sit for at least 10 minutes before serving.

3 large eggplants

3 tablespoons sea salt

2 cups Bob's Red Mill Gluten Free All-Purpose Baking Flour (or any brown rice flour)

2 tablespoons extra-virgin olive oil

3 cups Marinara Sauce (page 37)

4 cups Cashew Ricotta (page 33)

4 cups Cashew Mozzarella (soft, page 34)

½ cup Macadamia Parmigiano (page 35)

16 large fresh basil leaves

BREADED EGGPLANT PARMIGIANA

SERVES 4 TO 6

1 Cut the eggplant crosswise into about ¼-inch-thick circles.

2 Sprinkle the salt evenly over the eggplant and let it rest for 30 minutes.

3 After 30 minutes the eggplant should be covered in water. Wash off completely and gently pat dry with a clean dish towel or paper towel.

4 In a bowl, combine the egg replacer and cashew cream and whip until thick to make the batter.

5 Prepare two separate bowls, one with the batter and the other with the panko.

6 Dip each eggplant round one at a time into the batter, letting the excess drip off.

7 Next, roll the eggplant in the panko, making sure to completely coat it all the way around and on the ends as well. Set aside.

TIP: If you do not have panko, it is okay to use Pangrattato (page 51) for the breading!

Continued

2 large eggplants

2 tablespoons sea salt

2½ tablespoons egg replacer

4 cups Cashew Cream (page 56)

4 cups panko

Avocado oil, grapeseed oil, or rice bran oil for frying

2 cups Marinara Sauce (page 37)

1 cup melted Cashew Mozzarella (page 34)

1 tablespoon Macadamia Parmigiano (page 35)

3 to 4 fresh basil leaves, torn into small pieces

8   Fill a frying pan 1 inch deep with the oil.

9   Heat the oil to 360° to 375°F. Check the temperature with a deep-fry thermometer. The oil must be at least 350°F to fry the eggplant correctly.

10 Add the eggplant a few pieces at a time, making sure the slices are not touching or sticking together. Fry for 3 to 5 minutes, or until golden brown and crispy.

11 Remove the eggplant slices from the oil and place them on paper towels to drain.

12 If you prefer not to fry the eggplant, you can bake it: Preheat the oven to 375°F. Place the battered eggplant rounds on a well-oiled baking sheet. Bake for 30 minutes, flipping over halfway, until golden crispy brown.

13 Once your eggplant is cooked and ready to eat, let's dress it up!

14 Place the hot cooked eggplant on a serving platter and smother it with marinara sauce and cashew mozzarella, then sprinkle on the macadamia parmigiano and top with some basil.

EGGPLANT PARMIGIANA HERO

SERVES 2

I could tell you a thousand stories about my grandpa Enrico, although in America he was called Charlie. He died when I was seven years old, but I could tell you more tales about him than I could about people I see all the time. He was a truly special man, my idol, and my reason for wanting to open a restaurant and provide happiness through food.

Grandpa owned a sandwich shop called Punzone's Heroes in New York. A hero is what other people might refer to as a sub or a hoagie or a po'boy, but in New York it's called a hero: a big, Italian sandwich stuffed with a bunch of meats and tomatoes and lettuce. Grandpa was famous in the neighborhood for his shop, which was so busy he needed to get security to keep the line outside the door in order and only let a few people in at a time.

I thought Grandpa was the world's coolest person. He was always trying new things and took risks. For example, religious Catholics don't eat meat on Fridays, so on those days Grandpa wouldn't serve any meat sandwiches; instead it was always eggplant parm.

Loaf of Italian bread or a baguette

Extra-virgin olive oil for brushing

3-4 pieces of breaded eggplant (page 196)

1 cup Marinara Sauce (page 37)

1 cup melted Cashew Mozzarella (page 34)

2 teaspoons Macadamia Parmigiano (page 35)

3 or 4 fresh basil leaves, torn into small pieces

1   Cut an 8-inch-long piece of the bread or baguette, then slice the piece in half lengthwise.

2   Brush some olive oil on the inside of the bread slices. Toast them slightly to get some crunch.

3   Place your hot cooked eggplant inside the toasty bread and smother it with marinara sauce and cashew mozzarella. Sprinkle with macadamia parmigiano and top with the basil leaves.

4   Close the sandwich, cut in half (or into 4 pieces), and serve immediately.

MEATBALL PARMIGIANA HERO

SERVES 2

What else do I need to say—this is a classic!

---

1   Cut an 8-inch-long piece of the bread or baguette, then slice the piece in half lengthwise.

2   Brush some olive oil on the inside of the bread and toast it slightly to get some crunch.

3   Next, place your hot polpettine inside the toasty bread and smother with the marinara sauce and cashew mozzarella. Top with the macadamia parmigiano and basil leaves.

4   Close the sandwich, cut in half (or into 4 pieces), and serve immediately.

TIP: You can cut the meatballs in half to make the hero less bulky if needed. But I think more is better in this particular situation!

Loaf of Italian bread or a baguette

Extra-virgin olive oil for brushing

4 or 5 Polpettine (page 69)

2 cups Marinara Sauce (page 37)

1 cup melted Cashew Mozzarella (page 34)

1 tablespoon Macadamia Parmigiano (page 35)

3 to 4 fresh basil leaves, torn into small pieces

GRILLED TOFU PANINI,

aka ANGELICA'S PANINI

MAKES 1 PANINI

When I first became vegan, there were very few vegan restaurants, even in New York City. But in the East Village my mother and I found one, called Angelica's Kitchen, that offered wonderfully clean, vegan food. My mom took me there once a week, every week, throughout my teenage years and into my twenties.

One of my favorite menu items was the marinated tofu sandwich. It sounds boring, but it was excellent because it contained perfectly marinated tofu along with a walnut pesto and caramelized onions and carrots.

About the time when I opened Pura Vita in 2018, I received the devastating news that Angelica's Kitchen had closed. I quickly decided to come up with a version of that marinated tofu sandwich, calling it Angelica's Panini as a tribute.

½ tablespoon extra-virgin olive oil, plus more for brushing

½ tablespoon maple syrup

1 cup yellow onion cut into half-moons

1 cup thinly sliced carrots (use a mandoline)

¼ teaspoon sea salt

¼ teaspoon coriander

¼ teaspoon black pepper

1 loaf ciabatta

1 tablespoon Classic Pesto (page 38)

1 tablespoon Roasted Garlic Aioli (page 48)

4 pieces Grilled Citrus Herb Tofu (page 67)

½ cup wild arugula

1   Caramelize the onion and carrots: In a sauté pan, heat the olive oil over medium heat. Sauté the maple syrup, onion, and carrots with the salt, coriander, and pepper for at least 20 minutes, until the onion is light brown in color and the carrots are very soft. You can cook longer over lower heat to increase caramelization.

NOTE: This makes enough caramelized onions and carrots for 2 to 3 panini.

2   Now, let's panini: Slice the ciabatta lengthwise to open and make a proper sandwich. Brush some olive oil on the inside of the bread and toast slightly to get some crunch.

3   Slather the insides of your toasty ciabatta with a hearty dose of pesto on one side and roasted garlic aioli on the other side.

4   Place the hot grilled tofu on the bottom piece. Add ½ cup of the caramelized onions and carrots on the grilled tofu. Add the arugula on top of the onions and carrots.

5   Close the sandwich, cut in half (or into 4 pieces), and serve immediately.

SICILIAN TUNA MELT

MAKES 1 SANDWICH

With the perfect amount of warmth, crunch, melty mozzarella cheese, tangy capers, and a couple of fresh slices of juicy heirloom tomato, you might even trick a conventional tuna melt eater into loving this plant-based Sicilian version. If you want to take it up a notch, try adding some Calabrian chili paste to the toasted ciabatta.

One 4-inch square piece of ciabatta

Extra-virgin olive oil

1 tablespoon Roasted Garlic Aioli (page 48)

½ cup Tuna Salad (page 84)

2 tablespoons melted Cashew Mozzarella (page 34)

1 teaspoon capers in brine, drained

2 or 3 slices heirloom tomato

1   Slice the fresh ciabatta bread lengthwise to open and make a proper sandwich.

2   Preheat the oven to 350°F.

3   Brush some olive oil on the inside of the bread slices and toast slightly to get some crunch.

4   Slather the insides of your toasty ciabatta with a hearty amount of roasted garlic aioli.

5   Place the tuna salad on a baking sheet and bake for 6 to 8 minutes. Alternatively, you can scoop the tuna salad on a hot oiled griddle and cook for 5 to 6 minutes, flipping it over halfway.

6   Spoon the hot tuna on one half of the ciabatta.

7   Pour the melted cashew mozzarella on the tuna. Sprinkle capers on the mozzarella. Add the tomato slices.

8   Close the sandwich, cut in half (or into 4 pieces), and serve immediately.

GRILLED TOFU SPIEDINI

with SUMMER VEGETABLES

SERVES 4 TO 6

Spiedini means "skewers" in Italian, so this is basically an Italian kebab. To make it, you can skewer any type of marinated vegetable protein you'd like, such as tofu, tempeh, or seitan. This recipe uses tofu, but I recommend trying the other options as well. Then you add beautiful summer vegetables such as zucchini, tomatoes, eggplant, peppers, onion—again, whatever suits your fancy. This is one of the most satisfying dishes for vegans or meat eaters—very hearty, very savory, with that grilled taste everyone loves.

You will need skewers—stainless steel is preferred, but you can also use well-soaked bamboo skewers.

1 zucchini

1 summer squash

1 bell pepper, any color

½ red onion

1 teaspoon minced garlic

12 whole cherry tomatoes

¼ cup chopped fresh parsley, plus more for garnish

¼ cup extra-virgin olive oil, plus more (optional) for drizzling

2 cups Grilled Citrus Herb Tofu (page 67), cut into 1-inch cubes

Sea salt and black pepper

Pinch of Maldon salt for garnish

---

1   Wash the zucchini and summer squash, cut off the ends, then dice into 1-inch cubes. Wash the bell pepper and cut into 1 by 1-inch pieces. Peel and cut the red onion into 1 by 1-inch pieces.

2   In a large mixing bowl, combine the zucchini, summer squash, bell pepper, onion, garlic, and tomatoes with the parsley and olive oil. Marinate the vegetables at room temperature for 1 hour.

3   Assemble the spiedini. Each skewer should get at least 1 or 2 pieces of each vegetable, alternating the vegetables and the tofu. Mix it up!

4   Heat a ridged grill pan over medium-high heat for 3 to 5 minutes, or use a preheated outdoor grill with an open flame. (This is my preferred method.)

NOTE: The thickness of the sliced vegetables will determine the grilling time. Be sure to cut the vegetables evenly so they will cook in the same amount of time.

TIP: The parsley stalks provide an incredible amount of flavor, so feel free to chop them up and add them to the marinade as well.

5   Place the spiedini in a single layer in the pan or on the grill and cook for 3 minutes per side, or until lightly charred.

6   Season with salt and pepper to taste. Repeat until all the spiedini are grilled.

7   Transfer the skewers to a large serving dish and garnish with parsley, the Maldon salt, and a drizzle of olive oil, if using.

TIP: These spiedini are excellent served with Gremolata (page 45) or Pistachio Pesto (page 41) and Roasted Garlic Aioli (page 48).

RISOTTO POMODORO

SERVES 4 TO 6

Because risotto is typically a northern Italian dish, my family seldom made it. But as I was learning to cook, I ran into the misconception that it's impossible to make risotto vegan. Not true! Risotto is easily veganized, but you do have to have a lot of patience. You need to stand over the stove, dedicating your time to slowly stirring and stirring and stirring, adding the liquids little by little, so the dish comes out perfect.

    Then, you must eat it immediately!

1   Heat the olive oil, vegan butter, onion, shallots, celery, and garlic in a sauté pan and sauté over medium heat for 5 minutes.

2   Add the tomatoes and salt to the pan and simmer for 5 minutes.

3   Add the rice to the pan and sauté for 3 to 4 minutes.

4   Add the wine to the pan. Stir together, then simmer for 4 to 5 minutes, letting the alcohol burn off.

5   Slowly add small amounts of the vegetable broth to the pan as the rice is cooking. As it cooks, it will absorb all the liquid. Add the broth little by little, until all the liquid is used. Stir constantly until the rice is fully cooked al dente: tender, but with a bite.

6   Remove from the heat, add the melted vegan butter, and mix well. Add salt to taste.

¼ cup extra-virgin olive oil

½ cup salted vegan butter

1 cup finely diced yellow onion

1 cup finely diced shallots

1 cup finely diced celery

2 tablespoons minced garlic

2 cups mashed D.O.P. San Marzano tomatoes

2 teaspoons sea salt, plus more as needed

2 cups Arborio rice

1 cup dry white wine

1 cup vegetable stock

¼ cup melted vegan butter

HEARTBEET RISOTTO

SERVES 4 TO 6

This risotto recipe is perfect to impress your Valentine. The risotto will be deep magenta—which is connected to powerful feelings of love.

1 Heat the olive oil, vegan butter, onion, shallots, celery, and garlic in a sauté pan and sauté for 5 minutes.

2 Add the beets, salt, pepper, and sumac to the pan and sauté for 5 minutes.

3 Add the rice to the pan and sauté for 3 to 4 minutes.

4 Add the wine to the pan. Stir, then simmer for 4 to 5 minutes, letting the alcohol burn off.

5 Slowly add small amounts of the vegetable broth to the pan as the rice is cooking. As it cooks, it will absorb all the liquid. Add the broth little by little, until all the liquid is used. Stir constantly until the rice is fully cooked al dente: tender, but with a bite.

6 Remove from the heat, add the lemon juice and melted vegan butter, and mix well. Add salt to taste.

TIP: To dress up your Heartbeet Risotto, like I did in the photo on the next page, you can add microbasil and a few dollops of Almond Ricotta (page 35).

¼ cup extra-virgin olive oil

½ cup vegan butter

1 cup finely diced yellow onion

1 cup finely diced shallots

1 cup finely diced celery

2 tablespoons minced garlic

1 cup beets, roasted and pulsed in a blender until almost smooth

2 teaspoons sea salt, plus more as needed

1 teaspoon black pepper

1 tablespoon ground sumac

2 cups Arborio rice

1 cup dry red wine

4 cups vegetable stock

¼ cup lemon juice

¼ cup melted vegan butter

Heartbeet Risotto, *Page 207*

FRITTATA

(GLUTEN FREE)

SERVES 4 TO 6

A frittata is such a funny thing. It's basically an Italian version of an omelet, a dish that my family used to make to use up leftovers. Leftover pasta? Throw it in a frittata. Leftover vegetables? Throw them in a frittata. In fact, whatever's left over, you just chop it up (or don't chop it up) and throw it in. Super simple to make and delicious to eat! Nothing goes to waste.

---

1   Preheat the oven to 350°F.

2   In a medium bowl, combine the chickpea flour, water, ¼ cup of the olive oil, the garlic, rosemary, salt, and pepper. Whisk together until smooth. Let sit for 30 minutes.

3   Add the remaining 1 tablespoon of olive oil to a 1.5 to 2 quart cast-iron skillet. Using a brush or paper towel, coat the bottom and sides of the skillet with oil. Place the empty pan in the oven for 10 minutes to get the pan nice and hot. Remove the pan from the oven.

4   Pour the frittata base into the pan. Add the baby spinach, cashew mozzarella, and mushrooms. It is okay if these ingredients sink through the frittata base.

5   Top with the cherry tomatoes and a drizzle of olive oil.

6   Bake for 20 minutes, until the edges are golden-brown.

7   Once ready to serve, sprinkle with Maldon salt, pepper, and torn basil.

FRITTATA BASE

2 cups chickpea flour

2 cups filtered water

¼ cup extra-virgin olive oil, plus 1 tablespoon for the pan

2 teaspoons minced garlic

2 teaspoons chopped fresh rosemary leaves

2 teaspoons sea salt

½ teaspoon black pepper

FRITTATA MIX

½ cup baby spinach, cut into thin ribbons

2 tablespoons Cashew Mozzarella (page 34)

1 tablespoon chopped cremini mushrooms

½ cup halved cherry tomatoes

Extra-virgin olive oil for drizzling

Maldon salt for garnish

Freshly ground black pepper for garnish

Basil leaves, torn, for garnish

I
DOLCI

Chocolate Hazelnut Macaroons, *Page 225*

TIRAMISU

SERVES 6 TO 8

When I was very young, one of my favorite desserts was tiramisu. I loved the taste of the coffee, I loved that it was so creamy, I loved all its various layers. When I became vegan and realized I might never have tiramisu ever again, I was crushed—and vowed that someday I would figure out how to make it dairy free. So I did.

To make this tiramisu, you will need to buy either vegan ladyfingers or vegan vanilla cake (rather than the extra step of making them yourself, which, of course, you are welcome to do!).

1   Make the cashew mascarpone: Soak the cashews in water for at least 4 hours. Drain and rinse them well before using.

2   In a high-speed blender, combine the cashews, silken tofu, agave syrup, coconut oil, soy milk, vanilla paste, and salt. Blend until velvety smooth.

3   Transfer the mixture to a bowl and set aside in the refrigerator to solidify and cool to a temperature of 40°F.

4   In a medium bowl, whisk together the espresso, agave syrup, and rum.

5   Assemble the tiramisu: Layer the bottom of a 5 by 8-inch baking pan (at least 2 to 3 inches deep) with ladyfingers. Pour 1 cup of the espresso mixture over the ladyfingers to soak them completely. Add a 1-inch-thick layer of the mascarpone (using half of the mascarpone). Smooth the surface.

6   Add another layer of ladyfingers and pour the remaining espresso mixture over them and soak completely. Add a second 1-inch-thick layer of mascarpone. Smooth the surface.

7   Place the baking dish in the refrigerator to set for at least 4 hours before serving.

8   Top with cocoa powder to serve. Use a shaker or sifter for the cocoa powder so you can get an even cover without clumps.

CASHEW MASCARPONE

4 cups raw, unsalted cashews

Two 14-ounce packs silken tofu, drained

1 cup plus 2 tablespoons agave syrup

¾ cup refined coconut oil

1 cup unsweetened soy milk

1 tablespoon vanilla paste

½ teaspoon sea salt

ESPRESSO

16 ounces brewed, cold espresso

2 tablespoons agave syrup

¼ cup dark rum

TIRAMISU

Ladyfingers or vanilla cake

1 tablespoon Dutch-processed cocoa powder for dusting

ZEPPOLE

SERVES 4 TO 6

As a child, I loved going with my grandma to an Italian street fair (and in Brooklyn, there always seemed to be an Italian street fair somewhere). What I loved most about these events were the zeppole, doused in confectioners' sugar and sold in a brown paper bag, meaning that I (and everyone else) would walk around the fair reaching into the bag and pulling out treats as I went. Each zeppole was so covered with sugar that by the time I was done, I looked like a walking powdered doughnut.

When I became vegan, I cut zeppole out of my diet because of the dairy. But I knew I could veganize them, and I did! The good news is that they're quite easy to prepare—all that matters is good flour and good frying oil. When they're just right, zeppole are crunchy on the outside, soft and chewy on the inside.

When you're making zeppole, keep in mind that the oil temperature is vital. If the oil is too hot, the zeppole will burn on the outside and be raw on the inside. If the oil is not hot enough, the zeppole will not cook through and will turn into oily balls of dough.

2½ cups double zero flour (aka 00 flour or pasta fresca)

½ cup cane sugar

2 teaspoons fresh yeast

1⅓ cups warm filtered water

¼ cup extra-virgin olive oil

2 teaspoons baking powder

Pinch of sea salt

Avocado, grapeseed, or rice bran oil for frying

2 cups confectioners' sugar

TIP: I only use fresh yeast, as active dry yeast will not taste as pleasant. It's worth finding the fresh kind.

1   In the medium bowl of a stand mixer, combine the flour, sugar, yeast, water, olive oil, baking powder, and salt. Mix with a beater or whip attachment for 7 to 10 minutes, until creamy.

2   Let the dough rest at room temperature for 30 to 45 minutes.

3   Add about 2 inches of oil to a deep frying pan. Heat the oil to 360° to 375°F. Use a deep-fry thermometer to test.

4   Scoop out heaping tablespoon–size balls. Fry them in batches for 4 to 5 minutes, until golden. Do not crowd the pot.

5   While the balls are frying, place the confectioners' sugar in a medium mixing bowl. When the dough balls are fried to completion, toss them in the confectioners' sugar.

TIP: Be patient and don't immediately bite into the zeppole, or you will singe the roof of your mouth like I always do!

SANGUINACCIO

SERVES 4 TO 6

My grandmother on my father's side was from Calabria, a somewhat impoverished region of Italy. Her family could seldom afford to buy meat, but when they could, they would use every single part of that animal so as not to waste a morsel.

Fast-forward to when I was a little kid in New York. One year we were having a holiday dinner and my grandma put a dish on the table; it looked just like chocolate pudding.

I said, "Oh, chocolate!"

But when I went to take some, my father said, "No, no, no. Don't touch that."

"Why?" I asked. "It's chocolate pudding."

"No," he replied. "It is a pudding that has chocolate in it, but you wouldn't like it."

"But again, why?" I asked. "It's chocolate."

"It's not the kind of chocolate that you would like," he replied. I told him I liked every kind of chocolate, but he stuck to his guns and wouldn't elaborate.

I eventually discovered that my grandmother had made sanguinaccio, a type of chocolate pudding that uses pig's blood to create the pudding texture. That was their answer to using every single part of the animal whenever they got their hands on one.

It's not a surprise that I'm vegan!

1 cup Cashew Cream (page 56)

1¼ cups (200 grams 70 percent dark chocolate)

Pinch of sea salt

Pinch of cinnamon

1 tablespoon (10 grams) cornstarch

¼ cup blood orange juice (fresh if available, or non-blood orange juice is fine)

NOTE: If you have a kitchen scale, I recommend weighing out the 200 grams of chocolate exactly. With baking, precise measurements are important.

---

1   In a small saucepan over very low heat, heat the cashew cream, chocolate, salt, and cinnamon, stirring until smooth. Be careful not to turn up the heat, as this will make the fat separate from the cashew cream.

2   In a separate bowl, whisk the cornstarch into the blood orange juice and then pour it into the cashew cream and chocolate mixture.

3   Whisk continuously until the liquid starts to thicken.

4   Remove from the heat and let cool for 4 to 5 minutes before scooping into serving glasses.

PIGNOLI COOKIES

MAKES 2 DOZEN COOKIES

Pignoli (pine nuts) are a popular type of cookie originating in Naples and so, of course, they are popular in New York. My family always had pignoli on the table for every holiday.

8 ounces almond paste

¾ cup (or 1½ sticks) Earth Balance Vegan Buttery Sticks (softened at room temperature)

⅔ cup sugar

1 teaspoon almond extract

1 cup all-purpose flour

½ teaspoon baking powder

½ cup raw, unsalted shelled pignoli (pine nuts)

1   Preheat the oven to 350°F. Line a baking sheet with parchment paper.

2   In a large bowl, use an electric hand mixer to beat the almond paste, vegan butter, sugar, and almond extract until creamy.

3   Sift the flour and baking powder into the same bowl.

4   Using a spoon or your hands, combine the flour into the almond paste mixture until a smooth dough forms.

5   Pour the pignoli into a shallow bowl or dish.

6   Scoop out a 2-tablespoon-size piece of dough. Roll it into a ball between your palms. Gently push one side of the dough ball into the pine nuts to flatten it a little bit and to stick the nuts to it. Repeat with the rest of the dough.

7   Place the cookies on the baking sheet, pignoli-side up.

8   Bake for 12 to 15 minutes, until golden brown. Let cool on the baking sheet.

TIP: If you can find the soy-free Earth Balance Vegan Buttery Sticks, get those in place of the original. Some bakers have found that the flaxseed oil in the original recipe has a weird fishy taste.

PANNA COTTA

SERVES 4 TO 6

Panna cotta is a traditional Italian dessert normally made with heavy cream and gelatin. Yuck. We can do better. In this recipe, I replace the heavy cream with cashew and coconut creams, and replace the gelatin with agar-agar. It's surprising that most people don't even know what gelatin is (without getting too deep, let's just say it's disgusting). Agar-agar is made from algae and has an excellent ability to form gels. In the future, if you need to jelly up something, you will know where to turn once you follow this simple recipe!

1 cup (200 grams) coconut cream or canned full-fat coconut milk

2 tablespoons (20 grams) cornstarch

1 teaspoon (3 grams) agar-agar powder (not agar flakes)

1 cup Cashew Cream (page 56)

¼ cup (70 grams) cane sugar

1 tablespoon vanilla bean paste (I love Neilsen's)

Pinch of sea salt

8 teaspoons Raspberry Coulis (recipe follows)

NOTE: I'm including grams on this one because this recipe does require precision.

1   Chill the can of coconut cream in the refrigerator overnight. Make sure not to shake the can to maintain the separation of the cream and liquid. When you're ready to use it, remove the can of coconut cream from the refrigerator without tipping or shaking it. Carefully take off the lid and scrape out the top layer of the thickened cream and leave the liquid. Measure or weigh only the thickened cream (without the coconut water).

2   Add the cornstarch and agar-agar powder to a small bowl. Add ¼ cup of the cashew cream and stir well. Set aside.

3   Place the remaining ¾ cup cashew cream and the sugar in a saucepan over medium heat and stir for a couple of minutes until the sugar has dissolved.

4   Add the coconut cream, vanilla bean paste, and salt to the saucepan and continue to heat until the mixture simmers.

5   Add the cornstarch mixture to the saucepan and simmer for another 3 to 4 minutes, stirring continuously to ensure the mixture does not burn or stick to the bottom of the pan. The mixture will thicken to a runny custard consistency, forming the panna cotta.

6   Transfer to 4 to 6 individual glass bowls, cool to room temperature for about 15 minutes, then transfer to the refrigerator to set for 2 hours.

Continued

RASPBERRY COULIS

1   Add the frozen raspberries, agave syrup, and lemon juice to a high-speed blender and blend until smooth. Push the mixture through a chinois to remove all the raspberry seeds. The texture should be 100 percent smooth.

2   When the panna cotta has set, pour the raspberry coulis over it. Add a few (about three) whole fresh raspberries to the top of each panna cotta.

TIP: Do not try to make less coulis, as it will be more difficult to blend to perfection. You can freeze the leftover coulis and use it in other dishes and drinks.

RASPBERRY COULIS

1 pound frozen raspberries

1 cup agave syrup

½ teaspoon lemon juice

Fresh raspberries for topping

ALMOND MACAROONS

MAKES 4 DOZEN BITE-SIZE MACAROONS

Although chocolate anything is usually my favorite dessert, these almond macaroons are a close rival to their cocoa counterpart.

---

1 Preheat the oven to 350°F.

2 In a mixing bowl, combine the coconut, flour, maple syrup, vegan butter, vanilla bean paste, and salt.

3 Using a tablespoon scoop, portion the dough into small balls.

4 Place 3 almond slices, a drop of agave syrup, and a few flakes of Maldon salt on top of each macaroon.

5 Place on parchment-lined baking sheets and bake for 15 minutes, until firm but not hard. Remove from the oven, cool on the sheet, and store in an airtight container.

3 cups dried, unsweetened coconut

1¼ cups blanched almond flour (Bob's Red Mill is a great option)

1¼ cups maple syrup

⅓ cup softened vegan butter

1 tablespoon vanilla bean paste

½ teaspoon sea salt

½ cup sliced almonds for topping

Agave syrup for topping

Maldon salt for topping

CHOCOLATE HAZELNUT MACAROONS

MAKES 4 DOZEN BITE-SIZE MACAROONS

While they might not be famously Italian, the origins of coconut macaroons go all the way back to a medieval era of Italian culinary tradition. These little gems are super simple to make and have one of the cleanest ingredient lists you'll find in any dessert.

3 cups dried, unsweetened coconut

1¼ cups cocoa powder

1¼ cups maple syrup

⅓ cup softened vegan butter

1 tablespoon vanilla bean paste

½ teaspoon sea salt

2 cups hazelnuts for topping

Agave syrup for topping

Maldon salt for topping

1   Preheat the oven to 350°F.

2   In a mixing bowl, combine the coconut, cocoa powder, maple syrup, vegan butter, vanilla bean paste, and salt and mix well by hand.

3   Using a tablespoon scoop, portion the dough into small balls.

4   Place 3 hazelnuts, a drop of agave syrup, and a few flakes of Maldon salt on top of each macaroon.

5   Place the cookies on parchment-lined baking sheets and bake for 15 minutes, until firm but not hard. Remove from the oven, cool on the sheet, and store in an airtight container.

AFFOGATO

SERVES 1

This is gelato drowned in espresso—two of my favorite food groups together as one! On a hot summer day this is guaranteed to cool you down and pick you up all at the same time. An affogato is best eaten with a spoon before sipping the remaining espresso. If you are interested in adding yet another incredible layer, feel free to pour a shot of liqueur over the top. Frangelico is traditional, but be adventurous and try other options, such as amaretto or even dark rum.

1 to 2 scoops (about ½ cup) very cold vanilla or chocolate vegan gelato (or vegan ice cream if you cannot find vegan gelato)

1 double shot (2 ounces) hot espresso

1 tablespoon Frangelico, amaretto, or other liqueur (optional)

NOTE: If you don't have a Moka pot or an espresso machine, buy an espresso from the nearest coffee shop.

1   Chill a small bowl or glass in the freezer.

2   Place the gelato in the bowl, then slowly pour the hot espresso over the gelato.

3   Optional: Add a splash of Frangelico or try amaretto. The almond flavor is amazing here.

TIP: Make sure to eat this right away before the gelato completely melts!

LEMON MINT GRANITA

SERVES 2 TO 4

Granita is a semifrozen dessert originally from Sicily. It is related to sorbet, but reminds me more of a New York Italian ice, which was a daily summertime routine for me when I was a kid. Granita is cold and refreshing, always a perfect snack in the heat. This is a simple and easy way to cleanse your palate and enjoy a bit of light sweetness without the heavy fat content common to most frozen desserts.

¾ cup lemon juice

¾ cup agave syrup

4 cups filtered water

¼ bunch fresh mint, plus extra for serving

Lemon zest (optional)

1   In a high-speed blender on medium speed, blend the lemon juice, agave syrup, water, and mint together. The mint will turn the liquid slightly green.

2   Pour the liquid into a small metal loaf or square pan, leaving 2 to 3 inches above the liquid so it has room to expand. Place the pan in the freezer.

3   Allow to set for about 30 minutes. Remove the pan from the freezer and scrape the ice crystals from across the top of the frozen liquid and around the sides, to break them up. Return the pan to the freezer. Continue to scrape the ice crystals every 30 minutes for 4 hours.

4   Once the granita has reached a frozen yet spoon-able texture (similar to a soft sorbet), it is ready! You can leave the granita in the freezer until you're ready to serve it. If it gets too frozen to scoop out, leave it on the counter for 15 minutes to soften.

5   Divide among bowls. Top with fresh mint and lemon zest, if using.

COFFEE GRANITA

SERVES 2 TO 3

Coffee granita is a Sicilian favorite, perfect from morning to night. In Sicily, they eat this at breakfast with a fresh brioche!

2 cups hot espresso or strong coffee

1¼ cups cane sugar

Vegan whipped cream (optional)

1 Pour the hot espresso into a large bowl. Whisk in the sugar until it is completely dissolved. Allow to cool completely.

2 Pour the espresso into a small metal loaf or square pan, leaving 2 to 3 inches above the liquid so it has room to expand. Place the pan in the freezer.

3 Allow to set for about 30 minutes. Remove the pan from the freezer and scrape the ice crystals from across the top of the frozen liquid and around the sides, to break them up. Return the pan to the freezer. Continue to scrape the ice crystals every 30 minutes for 4 hours.

4 Once the granita has reached a frozen yet spoon-able texture (similar to a soft sorbet), it is ready! You can leave it in the freezer until you're ready to serve. If it gets too frozen to scoop out, leave it on the counter for 15 minutes to soften.

5 Transfer the granita to small serving dishes or glasses, top with vegan whipped cream, if using.

TIP: This is delicious served with fresh brioche!

SWEET SUMMER PEACHES *in* WHITE WINE

SERVES 2 TO 3

This one is all about my ma! Although she doesn't really enjoy drinking alcohol, when you throw in some fresh summer peaches, all bets are off. Summer peaches soaked in ice-cold white wine is an Italian cure-all for a hot summer day. My mom would say it's not really drinking, it's dessert, as she polished off the last peach slice and gulped down the remaining wine in her glass.

Make sure to refrigerate the peaches in wine for at least 5 to 6 hours. If you have time to prepare these ahead, they are even better the next day: the peaches and wine become one the longer they lie together.

4 to 5 ripe summer peaches

½ cup cane sugar, or more to taste

2 cups dry white wine (such as pinot grigio or pinot bianco)

½ teaspoon orange zest

---

1   Cut the peaches into ½- to ¾-inch-thin slices and place in a medium bowl.

2   Sprinkle them with the sugar. Gently stir.

3   Pour enough wine over the peach slices to fully submerge them. Stir gently.

4   Sprinkle the orange zest over the top and stir. Taste the liquid. Add additional sugar if desired.

5   Cover airtight and place the bowl in the refrigerator for a few hours or up to a day.

6   Serve the peaches in wineglasses with the wine. You will definitely want to sip the peach-infused wine after eating the peaches!

ACKNOWLEDGMENTS

I HAVE BEEN BLESSED THROUGHOUT MY LIFE, surrounded by those who love and support me unconditionally, even when my path seems to veer way off the well-traveled road.

My mother and father are first in this list. Even when you don't understand my thoughts and actions, you trust me and encourage me to carry forward. You do this with confidence, as if you know something about me that I don't even know. You have always been my biggest supporters, providing me with endless motivation to do what I am passionate about, regardless of anyone else's opinion. You are the very best parents any child could ever dream of. You are the reason I strive to always be better.

Thank you, Gene Stone. I never expected this experience to be such an incredible journey. In the beginning you were a total stranger, but before I could overthink, you began to guide me and managed to keep me focused in a way every mentor should. I have felt comforted and encouraged throughout this project. You have the perfect amount of patience and grace to pull out the very best from within my mind.

Nadia, my sister, my best friend, my partner, I could not, and I would not, want to do any of this without you. I waited thirty-five years of my life to find you. You are the light in the darkness. You make me a better person just by being next to me. Your spirit lifts me up and enables me to see over the chaos. Together, you and I could accomplish anything.

Serafin, you have taught me the deepest lessons about loyalty and trust. Thank you for the endless hours of recipe testing, making sure everything is always perfect. You have an amazing ability to understand me, even when I don't really understand myself. Your methods in our kitchen are an inspiration to me. I can simply say with confidence, this is "all your fault."

Rusty, thank you for your patience and encouragement. It has not always been easy for you with three restaurant openings and now this book distracting me, yet you remain my biggest fan. Your heartfelt support does not go unnoticed, even when I don't say it enough. You are strong, like a tree with its roots deep in the ground, and you provide safety for me when I need it most. I am grateful beyond words for the love we share.

Al, you are my chosen brother, my safe place. Anytime I am feeling down, you are always there to pick me up, dust me off, and remind me "who the fuck I am." Your honesty, strength, and kindness have guided me through many complicated moments of life. I am forever grateful to have you and your endless positive calming energy to lead us through this experience.

Neal, my first chef and mentor: Thank you for taking a chance on me, believing in me, and encouraging me to follow my passion in the kitchen. I do not know where I would be today if it were not for you and your incredible generosity and support. You gave me confidence and taught me how to be an amazing leader—just like you.

Tony, thank you for being an inspiring creative liaison since the very first day we worked together.

Roxy, thank you for being the ultimate social media superstar and for forcing me to dance, especially whenever I said no! You are always such a positive inspiration to me.

Anthony, thank you for showing me that anything is possible. You have broken boundaries in a way I have never witnessed before. You make me proud.

Paulie, thank you for busting my balls throughout my entire life. You made me strong enough to know that the more I am poked, the more committed I become. Anytime you've tasted my recipes and went back for another spoonful, I knew I was on to something great!

Vin, you believed I was a rock star ever since you were a little boy. Thank you for cheering me on since day one.

Thank you, Peter, for the endless years of friendship, talents, and creativity.

Thank you, Button, for your loving friendship and amazing artistic skills. Thank you for taking care of me and all the important details of Pura Vita. Thank you for always coming to visit me and being there when I need you most.

Thank you, Rick, for teaching me so much about myself. When I look at you, I see more than half a lifetime of travels and experiences that built me to be a stronger and more resilient woman.

Thank you, Cindy and Chris Derose, for all your contributions to Pura Vita and everything you do for the animals.

Ann, thank you for taking me in when I first moved to Los Angeles from Brooklyn.

John, aka "Badass Vegan," thank you for your endless motivation. Your positive energy is contagious. You gave me the confidence to make this book a reality.

Joanne, aka the "Korean Vegan," thank you for the inspiration to see this project through.

Howard Stern and Robin Quivers, thank you for teaching me that the most unlikely people can accomplish the most incredible things and break down stereotypes and boundaries, leading the way for others to do the same.

Edward and Val, thank you for the most incredibly beautiful styling and photography. Your talents and vision went beyond my expectations. Our time spent working together was pure joy and left me with an overwhelming sense of accomplishment.

Mia and Sarah, my agents, thank you for believing in me and this project.

Katherine Leak and the team from Rodale: Jenn Backe, Cassie Gitkin, Allie Fox, Lynn Wu, Lynne Yeamans, Samuel Wetzler, Martha Schwartz, Leda Scheintaub, Marisa Crumb, Mindy Fichter, Russell Powers, and Gina Gullinger.

Thank you to *VegOut* and *VegNews* magazines, which have shown me their undeniable support over the years.

To my Pura Vita family, thank you for being such an important part of this journey. I am so grateful to have all of you by my side, helping to make all my dreams come true day in and day out. The way we all take care of each other and love each other is the very reason for our success.

Thank you to my baby boys Eddie, Charlie, Louie, and Toni for providing me with the best kind of love on this earth.

Thank you to my grandparents for, well, everything. Thank you for cooking the most incredible foods. Thank you for teaching us all the joy of sharing with and taking care of our community. Thank you for coming to this country with the confidence to believe you could have the American dream. Thank you for providing our family with the deepest love that has carried through for several generations. Thank you for being from the south of Italy, where the very best food and wine in the world are created!

INDEX

A

Affogato, 226
Aged Sherry Vinaigrette, 97
    in Heirloom Tomato and
        Watermelon Salad, 100
    in Verde, 97
Aioli, Roasted Garlic, 48
Alfredo Sauce, 44
    in Baked Ziti Alfredo, 190
    in Fettuccine Alfredo, 170
Almond Ricotta, 33
    in Fresh Ravioli, 144–45
    in Heirloom Tomato and
        Watermelon Salad, 100
    in Pesto Calabrese, 39
    in Strawberry Almond Crostini,
        80
almonds
    Almond Macaroons, 223
    Almond Ricotta, 33
    Cesare Dressing, 94–96
    Classic Pesto, 38
    Peppas, 106
    Tuna Salad, 84
Arancini, 71–72
Arrabbiata Paste, 165
Artichokes, Stuffed, 116–19
arugula
    Grilled Tofu Panini aka Angelica's
        Panini, 202
    Tricolore, 93
    Verde, 97
asparagus
    Baked Ziti Alfredo, 190
    Grilled Summer Vegetables,
        121
    Roasted Lemon Asparagus,
        115
avocados
    Tuna Salad, 84
    Verde, 97

B

Baked Ricotta Served with Grilled
    Ciabatta, 60
Baked Ziti Alfredo, 190
Baked Ziti "Traditional", 189
balsamic glaze
    Caprese, 90
    Heirloom Tomato and
        Watermelon Salad, 100
    Strawberry Almond Crostini, 80
Balsamic Vinaigrette, 93
basil
    Breaded Eggplant Parmigiana,
        196–98
    Bruschetta, 64
    Caprese, 90
    Classic Pesto, 38
    Fusilli Primavera, 184
    Giambotta, 126
    Heirloom Tomato and
        Watermelon Salad, 100
    Marinara Sauce, 37
    Meatball Parmigiana Hero, 201
    Minestrone, 125
    Panzanella, 99
    Parmigiana di Melanzane, 195
    Penne alla Vodka, 181
    Pistachio Pesto, 41
    Roasted Garlic Cannellini Bean
        Dip, 86
    Strawberry Almond Crostini, 80
    Tagliatelle alla Bolognese,
        186–87
beans
    Cannellini Beans, 49
    Escarole and Beans, 128
    Gigante Beans, 68
    Minestrone, 125
    Pasta e Fagioli, 124
    Roasted Garlic Cannellini Bean
        Dip, 86
    Sautéed Swiss Chard with
        Cannellini Beans, 105
beets
    Heartbeet Risotto, 207
Belgian endive
    Tricolore, 93
bell peppers
    Calabrian Peppers and Potatoes,
        110
    Fusilli Primavera, 184
    Giambotta, 126
    Grilled Summer Vegetables, 121
    Grilled Tofu Spiedini with
        Summer Vegetables, 204–5
    Pesto Calabrese, 39
berries
    Raspberry Coulis, 222
    Strawberry Almond Crostini, 80
bread crumbs
    Baked Ziti Alfredo, 190
    Lemon Pepper Cream Paccheri
        with Spring Peas and
        Pistachio, 173–74
    Linguine di Mare in Garlic White
        Wine Sauce, 177–78
    Pangrattato (Italian Toasted
        Bread Crumbs), 51
    Roasted Lemon Asparagus, 115
    Spaghetti Aglio, Olio e
        Peperoncino, 159
    Stuffed Artichokes, 116–19
    Stuffed Mushrooms Oreganata,
        85
Breaded Eggplant Parmigiana,
    196–98
    in Eggplant Parmigiana Hero, 199
breads
    Bruschetta, 64
    Crostini, 79
    in Garlic Croutons, 55
    Grilled Ciabatta Garlic Bread, 54

in Pangrattato (Italian Toasted
Bread Crumbs), 51
in Panzanella, 99
Sicilian Tuna Crostini, 83
Strawberry Almond Crostini, 80
broccoli
Fusilli Primavera, 184
Roasted Winter Vegetables, 120
Broccoli Rabe, 102
Broccolini, Grilled, 109
Bruschetta, 64
Brussels sprouts
Candied Brussels Sprouts, 111
Roasted Winter Vegetables, 120
butternut squash
Butternut Cream Sauce, 175–76
Butternut Squash Bisque, 129

C

Cacio e Pepe, 161
Calabrian chili peppers
Calabrian Peppers and Potatoes,
110
Pesto Calabrese, 39
Sautéed Swiss Chard with
Cannellini Beans, 105
Spaghetti Aglio, Olio e
Peperoncino, 159
Calabrian Stuffed Cherry Peppers,
78
Candied Brussels Sprouts, 111
Cannellini Beans, 49
Escarole and Beans, 128
Minestrone, 125
Roasted Garlic Cannellini Bean
Dip, 86
Sautéed Swiss Chard with
Cannellini Beans, 105
Caprese, 90
Cashew Cream, 56
in Arancini, 71–72
in Breaded Eggplant Parmigiana,
196–98
in Crocchette di Patate, 76–77
in Panna Cotta, 221–22
in Penne alla Vodka, 181
in Roasted Garlic Creamy Tomato
Soup, 134
in Sanguinaccio, 217
Cashew Mascarpone, 214

Cashew Mozzarella, 34
in Arancini, 71–72
in Baked Ziti Alfredo, 190
in Baked Ziti "Traditional", 189
in Breaded Eggplant Parmigiana,
196–98
in Caprese, 90
in Crocchette di Patate, 76–77
in Eggplant Parmigiana Hero, 199
in Frittata, 211
in Gnocchi alla Sorrentina, 150
in Lasagna Pura, 155–56
in Meatball Parmigiana Hero, 201
in Parmigiana di Melanzane, 195
in Sicilian Tuna Melt, 203
in Spinach Ricotta Cannelloni,
153–54
Cashew Ricotta, 33
in Baked Ricotta Served with
Grilled Ciabatta, 60
in Baked Ziti Alfredo, 190
in Baked Ziti "Traditional", 189
in Fresh Ravioli, 144–45
in Lasagna Pura, 155–56
in Parmigiana di Melanzane, 195
in Pasta Pomodoro, 143
cashews
Alfredo Sauce, 44
Butternut Cream Sauce,
175–76
Cacio e Pepe, 161
Cashew Cream, 56
Cashew Mascarpone, 214
Cashew Mozzarella, 34
Cashew Ricotta, 33
Cesare Dressing, 94–96
Lemon Pepper Sauce, 173
Roasted Garlic Aioli, 48
Spinach Ricotta, 153–54
Tuna Salad, 84
Castelvetrano Olive Tapenade, 63
cauliflower
Roasted Heirloom Cauliflower,
112
Roasted Winter Vegetables, 120
Cesare, 94–96
Cesare Dressing, 94–96
cheese
Almond Ricotta, 33
Arancini, 71–72

Baked Ricotta Served with
Grilled Ciabatta, 60
Baked Ziti Alfredo, 190
Baked Ziti "Traditional", 189
Breaded Eggplant Parmigiana,
196–98
Caprese, 90
Cashew Mascarpone, 214
Cashew Mozzarella, 34
Cashew Ricotta, 33
Cesare, 94–96
Crocchette di Patate, 76–77
Eggplant Parmigiana Hero, 199
Fettuccine Alfredo, 170
Fresh Ravioli, 144–45
Frittata, 211
Fusilli Primavera, 184
Garlic Parmigiano Potato
Wedges, 75
Gnocchi alla Sorrentina, 150
Lasagna Pura, 155–56
Macadamia Parmigiano, 35
Meatball Parmigiana Hero, 201
Parmigiana di Melanzane, 195
Pasta e Ceci, 183
Pasta Pomodoro, 143
Pesto Cavatelli, 167
Sicilian Tuna Melt, 203
Spinach Ricotta Cannelloni,
153–54
Tagliatelle alla Bolognese,
186–87
Tricolore, 93
Cherry Peppers, Calabrian Stuffed,
78
chickpeas
Cesare, 94–96
Giambotta, 126
Minestrone, 125
Pasta e Ceci, 183
Chili Oil (Olio Santo, "Holy Oil"), 52
chocolate
Chocolate Hazelnut Macaroons,
225
Sanguinaccio, 217
Citrus Herb Tofu, Grilled, 67
Classic Pesto, 38
in Grilled Tofu Panini aka
Angelica's Panini, 202
in Pesto Cavatelli, 167

coconut
    Almond Macaroons, 223
    Chocolate Hazelnut Macaroons,
        225
coconut milk
    Butternut Squash Bisque, 129
    Panna Cotta, 221–22
Coffee Granita, 229
condiments
    Castelvetrano Olive Tapenade,
        63
    Chili Oil (Olio Santo, "Holy Oil"),
        52
    Gremolata, 45
    Olive Tapenade, 63
    Roasted Garlic Aioli, 48
    See also sauces
cookies
    Almond Macaroons, 223
    Chocolate Hazelnut Macaroons,
        225
    Pignoli Cookies, 218
cream
    Arancini, 71–72
    Breaded Eggplant Parmigiana,
        196–98
    Cashew Cream, 56
    Crocchette di Patate, 76–77
    Panna Cotta, 221–22
    Penne alla Vodka, 181
    Roasted Garlic Creamy Tomato
        Soup, 134
    Sanguinaccio, 217
Cremini Mushroom "Meat", 155
Crispy Sage, 176
Crocchette di Patate, 76–77
Crostini, 79
    Sicilian Tuna Crostini, 83
    Strawberry Almond Crostini, 80
Croutons, Garlic, 55

D

desserts
    Affogato, 226
    Almond Macaroons, 223
    Chocolate Hazelnut Macaroons,
        225
    Coffee Granita, 229
    Lemon Mint Granita, 228
    Panna Cotta, 221–22

Pignoli Cookies, 218
Sanguinaccio, 217
Sweet Summer Peaches in White
    Wine, 231
Tiramisu, 214
Zeppole, 216
dips and spreads
    Castelvetrano Olive Tapenade,
        63
    Olive Tapenade, 63
    Roasted Garlic Aioli, 48
    Roasted Garlic Cannellini Bean
        Dip, 86
    See also condiments; sauces
double zero flour
    Fresh Gnocchi, 148–49
    Fresh Pasta, 139–42
    Fresh Ravioli, 144–45
    Zeppole, 216
dressings
    Aged Sherry Vinaigrette, 97
    Balsamic Vinaigrette, 93
    Cesare Dressing, 94–96
    Red Wine Vinaigrette, 99

E

eggplants
    Breaded Eggplant Parmigiana,
        196–98
    Eggplant Parmigiana Hero, 199
    Giambotta, 126
    Parmigiana di Melanzane, 195
escarole
    Escarole and Beans, 128
    Italian Wedding Soup, 131
espresso
    Affogato, 226
    Coffee Granita, 229
    Tiramisu, 214

F

Fettuccine Alfredo, 170
Fresh Gnocchi, 148–49
Fresh Pasta, 139–42
Fresh Ravioli, 144–45
Fresno chilis
    Peppas, 106
Frittata, 211
Fusilli Primavera, 184

G

garlic
    Garlic Croutons, 55
    Garlic Parmigiano Potato
        Wedges, 75
    Grilled Ciabatta Garlic Bread, 54
    Linguine di Mare in Garlic White
        Wine Sauce, 177–78
    Olive Tapenade, 63
    Pesto Calabrese, 39
    Roasted Garlic, 46
    Roasted Garlic Aioli, 48
    Roasted Garlic Cannellini Bean
        Dip, 86
    Roasted Garlic Creamy Tomato
        Soup, 134
Garlic Croutons, 55
    in Cesare, 94–96
    in Panzanella, 99
    in Tricolore, 93
    in Verde, 97
gelato
    Affogato, 226
Giambotta, 126
Gigante Beans, 68
Gnocchi, Fresh, 148–49
Gnocchi alla Sorrentina, 150
granita
    Coffee Granita, 229
    Lemon Mint Granita, 228
green beans
    Minestrone, 125
Gremolata, 45
Grilled Broccolini, 109
Grilled Ciabatta Garlic Bread, 54
Grilled Citrus Herb Tofu, 67
    in Grilled Tofu Panini aka
        Angelica's Panini, 202
    in Grilled Tofu Spiedini with
        Summer Vegetables, 204–5
Grilled Summer Vegetables, 121
Grilled Tofu Panini aka Angelica's
    Panini, 202
Grilled Tofu Spiedini with Summer
    Vegetables, 204–5

H

Harden, Neal, 43
Hazelnut Macaroons, Chocolate,
    225

Heartbeet Risotto, 207
Heirloom Tomato and Watermelon
    Salad, 100

I

Italian Wedding Soup, 131

K

kale
    Cesare, 94–96
    Tagliatelle in Butternut Cream
        Sauce, 175–76
King Oyster Mushroom Stem
    Scallops, 177

L

Lasagna Pura, 155–56
lemons
    Lemon Mint Granita, 228
    Lemon Pepper Cream Paccheri
        with Spring Peas and
        Pistachio, 173–74
    Lemon Pepper Sauce, 173
    Roasted Lemon Asparagus,
        115
lentils
    Polpettine (Meatballs), 69–70
    Sicilian Red Lentil Soup, 132
    Tagliatelle alla Bolognese,
        186–87
    Umbrian Lentil Soup, 133
lettuce
    Cesare, 94–96
    Verde, 97
Linguine di Mare in Garlic White
    Wine Sauce, 177–78

M

Macadamia Parmigiano, 35
    in Breaded Eggplant Parmigiana,
        196–98
    in Cesare, 94–96
    in Eggplant Parmigiana Hero,
        199
    in Fettuccine Alfredo, 170
    in Fusilli Primavera, 184
    in Garlic Parmigiano Potato
        Wedges, 75
    in Meatball Parmigiana Hero, 201
    in Parmigiana di Melanzane, 195
    in Pasta e Ceci, 183
    in Pesto Cavatelli, 167

In Tagliatelle alla Bolognese,
    186–87
in Tricolore, 93
Marinara Sauce, 37
    in Baked Ziti "Traditional", 189
    in Breaded Eggplant Parmigiana,
        196–98
    in Eggplant Parmigiana Hero, 199
    in Gnocchi alla Sorrentina, 150
    in Lasagna Pura, 155–56
    in Parmigiana di Melanzane, 195
    in Pasta Pomodoro, 143
    in Penne all'Arrabbiata, 165
    in Spaghetti alla Puttanesca, 162
    in Spinach Ricotta Cannelloni,
        153–54
    in Tagliatelle alla Bolognese,
        186–87
Marinated Olives, 62
Mascarpone, Cashew, 214
Meatball Parmigiana Hero, 201
Minestrone, 125
mint
    Gremolata, 45
    Lemon Mint Granita, 228
Mozzarella. Cashew, 34
mushrooms
    Cremini Mushroom "Meat", 155
    Frittata, 211
    King Oyster Mushroom Stem
        Scallops, 177
    Linguine di Mare in Garlic White
        Wine Sauce, 177–78
    Polpettine (Meatballs), 69–70
    Stuffed Mushrooms Oreganata,
        85

O

olives
    Castelvetrano Olive Tapenade,
        63
    Marinated Olives, 62
    Olive Tapenade, 63
    Spaghetti alla Puttanesca, 162
orange juice
    Sanguinaccio, 217

P

Pangrattato (Italian Toasted Bread
    Crumbs), 51
    in Baked Ziti Alfredo, 190

in Lemon Pepper Cream
    Paccheri with Spring Peas and
    Pistachio, 173–74
in Linguine di Mare in Garlic
    White Wine Sauce, 177–78
in Roasted Lemon Asparagus,
    115
in Spaghetti Aglio, Olio e
    Peperoncino, 159
in Stuffed Mushrooms
    Oreganata, 85
panko
    Arancini, 71–72
    Breaded Eggplant Parmigiana,
        196–98
    Crocchette di Patate, 76–77
Panna Cotta, 221–22
Panzanella, 99
Parmigiana di Melanzane, 195
Parmigiano, Macadamia, 214
parsley
    Cremini Mushroom "Meat", 155
    Crocchette di Patate, 76–77
    Fusilli Primavera, 184
    Giambotta, 126
    Gremolata, 45
    Grilled Tofu Spiedini with
        Summer Vegetables, 204–5
    Minestrone, 125
    Olive Tapenade, 63
    Pasta e Ceci, 183
    Polpettine (Meatballs), 69–70
    Sicilian Tuna Crostini, 83
    Spaghetti Aglio, Olio e
        Peperoncino, 159
    Stuffed Artichokes, 116–19
    Stuffed Mushrooms Oreganata,
        85
    Tagliatelle alla Bolognese,
        186–87
    Tuna Salad, 84
pasta
    al dente cooking, 27
    Baked Ziti Alfredo, 190
    Baked Ziti "Traditional", 189
    Cacio e Pepe, 161
    Fettuccine Alfredo, 170
    Fresh Gnocchi, 148–49
    Fresh Pasta, 139–42
    Fresh Ravioli, 144–45

Fusilli Primavera, 184
Gnocchi alla Sorrentina, 150
Italian Wedding Soup, 131
pasta (continued)
    Lasagna Pura, 155–56
    Lemon Pepper Cream Paccheri
        with Spring Peas and
        Pistachio, 173–74
    Linguine di Mare in Garlic White
        Wine Sauce, 177–78
    machines, 28
    pasta di Gragnano, 23
    Pasta e Ceci, 183
    Pasta e Fagioli, 124
    Pasta Pomodoro, 143
    Penne alla Vodka, 181
    Penne all'Arrabbiata, 165
    Pesto Calabrese with Bucatini,
        168
    Pesto Cavatelli, 167
    shapes, 24
    Spaghetti Aglio, Olio e
        Peperoncino, 159
    Spaghetti alla Puttanesca, 162
    Spinach Ricotta Cannelloni,
        153–54
    Tagliatelle alla Bolognese,
        186–87
    Tagliatelle in Butternut Cream
        Sauce, 175–76
    water, 28–29
Pasta e Ceci, 183
Pasta e Fagioli, 124
Pasta Pomodoro, 143
Peaches, Sweet Summer, in White
    Wine, 231
peas
    Fusilli Primavera, 184
    Lemon Pepper Cream Paccheri
        with Spring Peas and
        Pistachio, 173–74
Penne alla Vodka, 181
Penne all'Arrabbiata, 165
peperoncino
    Chili Oil (Olio Santo, "Holy Oil"),
        52
    Spaghetti Aglio, Olio e
        Peperoncino, 159
pepitas
    Peppas, 106

Spiced Pepitas, 57
Peppas, 106
pesto
    Classic Pesto, 38
    Pesto Calabrese, 39
    Pesto Calabrese with Bucatini,
        168
    Pesto Cavatelli, 167
    Pistachio Pesto, 41
Pignoli Cookies, 218
pistachios
    Lemon Pepper Cream Paccheri
        with Spring Peas and
        Pistachio, 173–74
    Pistachio Pesto, 41
    Roasted Pistachio Crumble, 42
Polpettine (Meatballs), 69–70
    in Italian Wedding Soup, 131
    in Meatball Parmigiana Hero,
        201
potatoes
    Calabrian Peppers and Potatoes,
        110
    Crocchette di Patate, 76–77
    Fresh Gnocchi, 148–49
    Garlic Parmigiano Potato
        Wedges, 75
    Giambotta, 126
    Gnocchi alla Sorrentina, 150
    Italian Wedding Soup, 131
    Minestrone, 125
pumpkin seeds. See pepitas

R
radicchio
    Tricolore, 93
Raspberry Coulis, 222
Red Wine Vinaigrette, 99
rice
    Arancini, 71–72
    Heartbeet Risotto, 207
    Risotto Pomodoro, 208
ricotta
    Almond Ricotta, 33
    Cashew Ricotta, 33
    in Fresh Ravioli, 144–45
    Spinach Ricotta, 153–54
    See also Almond Ricotta;
        Cashew Ricotta
Risotto Pomodoro, 208

Roasted Garlic, 46
    in Olive Tapenade, 63
    in Pesto Calabrese, 39
    in Roasted Garlic Aioli, 48
    in Roasted Garlic Cannellini Bean
        Dip, 86
    in Roasted Garlic Creamy Tomato
        Soup, 134
Roasted Garlic Aioli, 48
    in Grilled Tofu Panini aka
        Angelica's Panini, 202
    in Sicilian Tuna Melt, 203
Roasted Garlic Cannellini Bean
    Dip, 86
Roasted Garlic Creamy Tomato
    Soup, 134
Roasted Heirloom Cauliflower, 112
Roasted Lemon Asparagus, 115
    in Baked Ziti Alfredo, 190
Roasted Pistachio Crumble, 42
    in Heirloom Tomato and
        Watermelon Salad, 100
    in Lemon Pepper Cream
        Paccheri with Spring Peas and
        Pistachio, 173–74
    in Roasted Heirloom Cauliflower,
        112
Roasted Winter Vegetables, 120

S
Sage, Crispy, 176
salads
    Caprese, 90
    Cesare, 94–96
    Heirloom Tomato and
        Watermelon Salad, 100
    Panzanella, 99
    Tricolore, 93
    Tuna Salad, 84
    Verde, 97
sandwiches
    Eggplant Parmigiana Hero, 199
    Grilled Tofu Panini aka Angelica's
        Panini, 202
    Meatball Parmigiana Hero, 201
    Sicilian Tuna Melt, 203
Sanguinaccio, 217
sauces
    Alfredo Sauce, 44
    Butternut Cream Sauce, 175–76

Classic Pesto, 38
Gremolata, 45
Lemon Pepper Sauce, 173
Marinara Sauce, 37
Pesto Calabrese, 39
Pistachio Pesto, 41
Raspberry Coulis, 222
Sautéed Spinach, 103
Sautéed Swiss Chard with
    Cannellini Beans, 105
semolina flour
    Fresh Pasta, 139–42
    Fresh Ravioli, 144–45
Sicilian Red Lentil Soup, 132
Sicilian Tuna Crostini, 83
Sicilian Tuna Melt, 203
soups
    Butternut Squash Bisque, 129
    Escarole and Beans, 128
    Giambotta, 126
    Italian Wedding Soup, 131
    Minestrone, 125
    Pasta e Fagioli, 124
    Roasted Garlic Creamy Tomato
        Soup, 134
    Sicilian Red Lentil Soup, 132
    Umbrian Lentil Soup, 133
soy milk
    Cashew Mascarpone, 214
Spaghetti Aglio, Olio e
    Peperoncino, 159
Spaghetti alla Puttanesca, 162
Spiced Pepitas, 57
    in Tagliatelle in Butternut Cream
        Sauce, 175–76
    in Verde, 97
spinach
    Frittata, 211
    Italian Wedding Soup, 131
    Minestrone, 125
    Pasta e Ceci, 183
    Sautéed Spinach, 103
    Spinach Ricotta, 153–54
    Umbrian Lentil Soup, 133
Spinach Ricotta, 153–54
    in Fresh Ravioli, 144–45
    in Spinach Ricotta Cannelloni,
        153–54
Spinach Ricotta Cannelloni,
    153–54

squash
    Butternut Cream Sauce, 175–76
    Butternut Squash Bisque, 129
    Grilled Summer Vegetables, 121
    Grilled Tofu Spiedini with
        Summer Vegetables, 204–5
    Roasted Winter Vegetables, 120
Stern, Howard, 43
Strawberry Almond Crostini, 80
Stuffed Artichokes, 116–19
Stuffed Mushrooms Oreganata, 85
Sweet Summer Peaches in White
    Wine, 231
Swiss Chard, Sautéed, with
    Cannellini Beans, 105

T
Tagliatelle alla Bolognese, 186–87
Tagliatelle in Butternut Cream
    Sauce, 175–76
terms, 27–29
Tiramisu, 214
tofu
    Cashew Mascarpone, 214
    Cashew Ricotta, 33
    Grilled Citrus Herb Tofu, 67
    Grilled Tofu Panini aka Angelica's
        Panini, 202
    Grilled Tofu Spiedini with
        Summer Vegetables, 204–5
    Spinach Ricotta, 153–54
tomatoes
    Bruschetta, 64
    Caprese, 90
    D.O.P. San Marzano, 21
    Frittata, 211
    Fusilli Primavera, 184
    Giambotta, 126
    Grilled Tofu Spiedini with
        Summer Vegetables, 204–5
    Heirloom Tomato and
        Watermelon Salad, 100
    Marinara Sauce, 37
    Minestrone, 125
    Panzanella, 99
    Pasta e Fagioli, 124
    Pasta Pomodoro, 143
    Penne alla Vodka, 181
    Penne all'Arrabbiata, 165
    Pesto Cavatelli, 167

Risotto Pomodoro, 208
    Roasted Garlic Creamy Tomato
        Soup, 134
    Sicilian Tuna Crostini, 83
    Sicilian Tuna Melt, 203
    Spaghetti alla Puttanesca, 162
tomatoes, sun-dried
    Pasta e Ceci, 183
    Pesto Calabrese, 39
tools, 27–29
Tricolore, 93
Tuna Salad, 84
    in Calabrian Stuffed Cherry
        Peppers, 78
    in Sicilian Tuna Crostini, 83
    in Sicilian Tuna Melt, 203

U
Umbrian Lentil Soup, 133

V
vegetables
    Grilled Summer Vegetables, 121
    Grilled Tofu Spiedini with
        Summer Vegetables, 204–5
    Roasted Winter Vegetables, 120
    See also specific vegetables
Verde, 97

W
Watermelon Salad, Heirloom
    Tomato and, 100
wine, red
    Heartbeet Risotto, 207
wine, white
    Arancini, 71–72
    Linguine di Mare in Garlic White
        Wine Sauce, 177–78
    Risotto Pomodoro, 208
    Sweet Summer Peaches in White
        Wine, 231

Y
Yam Croutons, 96

Z
Zeppole, 216
zucchini
    Giambotta, 126
    Grilled Summer Vegetables, 121
    Grilled Tofu Spiedini with
        Summer Vegetables, 204–5

ABOUT THE AUTHORS

CHEF TARA PUNZONE is an Italian American from New York who has thrived on a vegan diet for more than thirty years. Her passion for healthy southern Italian food has been evolving since her childhood when she made the decision to adopt a vegan lifestyle. It was also at that time when Tara began converting all her family's traditional dishes to vegan versions of the same, without compromise.

In 2018, Tara opened Pura Vita West Hollywood, the first 100-percent plant-based Italian restaurant and wine bar in the country. At Pura Vita she has created a unique dining experience that has the ambiance of a New York City wine bar with a traditional menu reflecting the best of southern Italy—all of it plant-based.

Pura Vita has won numerous awards, including the National Veggie Awards for "Best Italian Restaurant" in the country from *VegNews* magazine three years in a row, 2021, 2022, and 2023, and *Easy Reader*'s Best of the Beach "Best Vegan Restaurant" in 2022 and 2023.

Tara is also the winner of the National Award for "Chef of the Year" by *VegOut* magazine.

GENE STONE has written fifty books on a wide variety of subjects, but for the last two decades he has concentrated on writing books (either under his own name, as a co-writer, or as a ghostwriter) about plant-based diets and their relationship to animal protection, health, and the environment. Among these are such titles as *Forks Over Knives, 72 Reasons to Be Vegan, How Not to Die, The How Not to Die Cookbook, Living the Farm Sanctuary Life, Rescue Dogs, Eat for the Planet, Eat for the Planet Cookbook, Mercy for Animals, The Awareness, The Engine 2 Diet, Plant-Strong,* and *Animalkind.*